If I
Perish

If I
Perish

FACING
IMPRISONMENT,
PERSECUTION
AND DEATH, A
YOUNG KOREAN
CHRISTIAN DEFIES
THE JAPANESE
WARLORDS.

ESTHER AHN KIM

MOODY PRESS
CHICAGO

© 1977 by
MOODY BIBLE INSTITUTE

All scripture quotations, unless otherwise indicated, are taken from the American Standard Version of the Bible.

Scripture quotations marked NASB are taken from the New American Standard Bible®, © Copyright The Lockman Foundation 1960, 1962, 1963, 1968, 1971, 1972, 1973, 1975, 1977. Used by permission.

Library of Congress Cataloging-in-Publication Data

Kim, Esther Ahn.
    If I perish.
    Translation of Chugumyon chugurita.
    1. Kim, Esther Ahn. 2. Women—Korea—Biography. I. Title
    ISBN 0-8024-3079-1
    CT1848.A49A313 365'.6'0925 [B] 76-49627

1 3 5 7 9 10 8 6 4 2

Printed in the United States of America

CONTENTS

PUBLISHER'S PREFACE

The recent upsurge in reader interest in events and experiences of the Second World War years has resulted in a spate of books focusing on Nazi and Soviet torture and concentration camp experiences. Yet during these years, thousands of Korean Christians were undergoing harassment, imprisonment, and torture as brutal and ingenious as any carried out by Roman emperors or during the Inquisition.

Convinced that God had called them, Ahn Ei Sook, a wealthy industrialist's frail daughter and Christian school teacher, and Elder Park, a Methodist spiritual leader, set out in 1939 on an incredible journey from Pyongyang to Tokyo to make Japanese leaders aware of .Japanese atrocities against Korean Christians and warn them of God's judgment by fire from the sky. Prepared to die for their audacious penetration of the sacrosanct Japanese Diet, they instead went to prison. Miss Ahn's courageous activities in prison not only brought the light of the Gospel to many, but also resulted in a reduction of torture.

After Ahn Ei Sook was released from prison, she was married to Don Kim. Eventually they toured the United States and Europe to tell about God's sustaining power during six harrowing but triumphant years in Japanese prisons (1939–1945). Her experiences were published as a book in Korea in 1967, which quickly became the all-time religious best-seller in Korea. Published in Japanese in 1973, the book became a national sensation, being entered into Japan's national library as well as becoming number three on the all-time religious best-seller list. Japanese Christians raised the funds and produced a film based on the book.

FOREWORD

I had resolved to die a martyr, but I had failed. As I saw so many dearly beloved Christian leaders perish under the cruel persecution, how I wept and cried out to my God.

"O Lord, this moment send Your heavenly cameras to take pictures of this cruelty. Hurry, please!"

I truly believe that He took pictures of everything that happened during those terrible years. At the same time He helped me to remember the details and facts of every event: how Jesus loved those who loved Him; how He gave them strength to overcome the power of darkness; and how, in His unfailing mercy, He helped believers to have faith in Him. I, too, knew His love and strength and peace. I would share it all with you but my pen is imperfect. I cannot explain how such a weak woman as I was given such wonderful blessings during times of fear and suffering.

This is the record of my prison life and a testimony of the acts of Jesus Christ. It is my earnest prayer that the glory of Jesus be manifested.

"Jesus, let me offer this humble testimony to You. I love You with my all."

MRS. DON M. KIM
(MAIDEN NAME: AHN EI SOOK)

1

DECLARATION OF WAR AT NAMSAN MOUNTAIN

It was the first of the month, the day appointed by our Japanese oppressors as the time for the mass pilgrimage to the shrine where we had been commanded to go and worship. At the Christian school where I taught music, all the girls were summoned to the playground. On orders from the principal, teachers were scurrying about, seeking those who had hidden themselves in classrooms and rest rooms in the vain hope that they might be spared the indignity and blasphemy of bowing before the shrine.

Looking down on the noisy confusion below, I felt like crying, but the tears would not come. I threw myself to the floor and with much sadness began to tell Jesus about it. Suddenly the sharp staccato of footsteps approached down the hall outside the door and I heard a stern, familiar voice.

"Miss Ahn! Are you there?" It was the principal. She had come to look for me herself. In silence I got up and opened the door. She was glaring at me, anger smoldering in her taut features. "Today is the first of the month."

As if I didn't know.

"We have to take the girls up the mountain to the shrine," she informed me. "Remember?"

Our eyes met and fought silently.

"You are not the only believer," the principal said, her voice rasping with tension. "This is a Christian school. Most of the pupils are Christians. So are all the other teachers. Even *I* am a Christian!"

I remained silent.

"Think about it, Miss Ahn. Is there any believer in Christ who *wants* to bow to heathen gods? We all hate to do such a thing, but we Christians are being persecuted with a power too ruthless to stand against. Unless we worship at the Japanese shrine, they will close this school!"

All of this I knew, and it troubled me deeply. The Japanese conquerors of our beloved Korea debased God and blasphemed our Lord Jesus Christ. Anyone who refused to bend his knee in the Japanese shrines—whether missionary, pastor, or deacon—was mercilessly tortured once he was found out. His fate was that of a traitor.

As the school principal this woman was responsible for the actions of the teachers and pupils, so I could understand her concern. But had she forgotten the words of Christ: "I am the way, and the truth, and the life" (John 14:6)?

Persecution had not just begun today. Across Korea, many Christians had already given their lives because they would not be swayed from their faith in Christ. Now the same kind of persecution had fallen upon our city and our little school. I knew why the principal wanted to force us all to go to the shrine, but I could not understand how she could have reached such a decision. I did not know why she would go directly against the Word of God by compromising with idolatry.

She must have sensed my disapproval. "You can see what great trouble you will cause this school if you fail to cooperate," she continued. For the first time I thought I caught a note of hatred in her voice. "But you don't seem to care about that. You are thinking only of yourself."

"If you want me to go to the mountain, I will," I told her, leaving the quiet safety of my music room and going down the stairs ahead of her.

"And you will worship at the shrine, Miss Ahn," she called out as she hurried after me. "Right?"

I had no answer for her. The girls were eyeing me in bewilderment and dismay, for they had not expected me to yield to the principal's orders. Taking my place at the head of the column, we started on the long trek to the mountain shrine. I could hear the small voices of the girls as they whispered behind me.

"Even Miss Ahn is going," they said. "Now God will surely look over us!"

"Our principal has such power! She has made Miss Ahn go to the shrine!"

"It is the fear of the police that has broken her."

I looked up into the sky and thought of Daniel. We in Korea were facing the same sort of idolatry which Daniel had resisted. The Japanese had built shrines in all the cities and villages of our captive land, forcing our people to place miniature shrines in every school, government office, and household. Then had come the latest blasphemy. Shrines were placed in every Christian church, and police were dispatched to every service to see that every person who came bowed to the pagan god before the worship service.

Pastors were a special target. If a minister of the Gospel opposed the worship at the newly erected shrine, or revealed what the policeman interpreted as a haughty attitude toward him, he was hauled to the police station and subjected to indescribable torture. But the persecution did not stop there. The food ration was immediately taken from the new prisoner's family, leaving them to starve. It was easy to see why most Koreans hated the Japanese and cursed them as devils.

I probably knew more about the Japanese than the average Korean. In spite of the fact that my mother was a fine Christian and wanted me to attend a nearby mission school, my unbelieving father insisted on sending me to a public school where I was given a Japanese education. When I graduated from high school, Mother wanted to send me to a Christian school in America. My father would not listen.

"She cannot succeed in life here unless she learns the Japanese ways," he said. "She will finish her education in Japan."

When I first returned to Korea after my graduation in Japan, I found life pleasant enough. I got a job teaching at a public girls' school. But the Japanese principal's manner was so arrogant and proud that I changed jobs and began to teach at the mission school.

Then this shrine worship was imposed upon *us*.

At first I managed to escape it through one ruse or another, but even as I did, I knew I could not keep that up forever. The war between China and Japan increased in intensity, and a new religious zeal seized the Japanese authorities. They were going to make sure that everyone in Korea, and especially we Christians, worshiped at the feet of their gods.

As we made our way up the mountain, I fixed my gaze on the vast sky beyond the hills and within myself repeated the words of Shadrach, Meshach, and Abednego which they had spoken to the Babylonian king, Nebuchadnezzar.

"But if not" (Daniel 3:18, italics added).

Even if God did not save them from the burning fire, they were saying, they would die honoring Him. I was going to make that same decision. With God's help, I would never bow before the Japanese idol, even if He did not save me from the hands of the Japanese. I was saved by Jesus. I could bow only before God, the Father of my Savior. I felt as though I could already see the burning furnace yawning for me.

While we walked I was praying. I knew what I was going to do. "Today on the mountain, before the large crowd," I told myself, "I will proclaim that there is no other God beside You. This is what I will do for Your holy name."

Peace filled my heart and I was surprised to find that I felt like singing. My heart was as broad as the ocean, and even the clouds seemed friendly to me. I wondered if the saints who had been persecuted and killed for the sake of the Gospel would be looking at me. I was not going to live my youthful life for myself. I would offer it to the Lord and bear witness of Him. I was filled with happiness for having been born in this age of bitterness.

"My sheep hear My voice," I recited aloud from chapter 10 of the Gospel of John, "and I know them, and they follow Me; and I give eternal life to them, and they shall never perish; and no one shall snatch them out of My hand. My Father, who has given them to Me, is greater than all; and no one is able to snatch them out of the Father's hand. I and the Father are one" (vv. 27–30 NASB).

When we finally reached the shrine, a great crowd already had gathered. Probably a dozen schools were represented, their pupils standing in straight, respectful lines, not daring to whisper or to move from their positions. Because I had been so reluctant to come, our school was the last to arrive. Everyone was looking at us, especially the disapproving Japanese policemen.

I was like a child at the shrine, afraid even to make a noise because of the police officers. As a sense of uneasiness swept over me, I tried to pray, but my prayers were too weak. I recited the Lord's Prayer three times, and closing my eyes, I stammered out my own lack of courage and strength.

"O Lord," I prayed, "I am so weak! But I am Your sheep so I must obey and follow You. Lord, watch over me."

Again I went back to chapter 10 of John. "My sheep hear My voice, and I know them, and they follow Me" (10:27). Didn't Jesus say He knew me and would watch over me? I was still determined to testify honestly and openly that I was His follower.

"Attention!" A strident order shrilled above the murmuring of the crowd. The people straightened, line by line. We were accustomed to being subservient, for we had been the captives of the Japanese for more than thirty-seven years. "Our profoundest bow to Amaterasu Omikami [the sun-goddess]!"

As one person, that enormous crowd followed the shouted order by bending the upper half of their bodies solemnly and deeply. Of all the people at the shrine, I was the only one who remained erect, looking straight at the sky. Moments before, uneasiness and fear had troubled my heart, but now they were completely gone. I was quite calm. My conscience whispered to me, "You have fulfilled your responsibility."

As I walked behind the freshman class, I talked once more to Jesus. "Everything is finished now. I have done what I should have done. I commit the rest to You. Now the only way left for me is to hear and follow You."

My mind was like that of a general who had just declared war, but as we made our way back to the school my heart was overshadowed by a dark cloud.

Everyone had seen me refuse to bow to the shrine. I would be dragged to the police station and kicked and beaten until my eyes would come out. Even as a child I had never been so much as scolded.

I wondered if I could stand being whipped and hearing those swaggering men blaspheme the name of Jesus.

I could honestly say I was not afraid of dying, but I feared being tortured without dying. How long could this body endure? What if I gave up my faith under the relentless torture? Just thinking of it made me so faint I could hardly see where I was walking.

But I could not retreat. I had to fight. But, I was a sinner and so very weak. What could I do? I wished I could have ended my life at that moment, even before we got back to the school.

"Let not your heart be troubled," Jesus was saying to me. "Believe in God, believe also in me. . . . I will not leave you desolate. . . . Peace I leave with you; my peace I give unto you. . . . Let not your heart be troubled, neither let it be fearful" (John 14:1, 18, 27).

A light was turned on in the darkness of my heart. The

clouds and patches of blue sky were smiling at me, and a song came to mind.

> Did we in our own strength confide,
>   Our striving would be losing;
> Were not the right Man on our side,
>   The Man of God's own choosing:
> Dost ask who that may be?
>   Christ Jesus, it is He; Lord Sabaoth His Name,
> From age to age the same,
>   And He must win the battle.
>
> MARTIN LUTHER

I felt as though I had been listening to Martin Luther in his battle for truth. He, too, lived during a dark day for Christians, when massacre and persecution were at their height. He was a scholar and a man of great character. *But what am I?* I thought. *I am an unknown, powerless young woman.*

I felt that the apostle Paul must have had times when he experienced the same problems I faced. I drew strength from what he wrote about them. "For when I am weak, then am I strong" (2 Corinthians 12:10).

"Oh Lord," I prayed, "let it come!"

2

ESCAPE!

The full force of my act of defiance at the shrine rushed over me. It had not been done in the safety of my room. I had refused to pay homage to the Japanese goddess before a great throng of people. Even the students saw what I had done. Concern darkened their loyal young faces. It was not for themselves that they were afraid; it was for me. They walked in silence, glancing back occasionally as though it might be their last opportunity to see me.

I had no fear for myself, but I was well aware of my critical situation. *I am dead,* I realized. *Ahn Ei Sook died today at mountain Namsan.*

In the few minutes since we had left the shrine, the scattered blue of the sky disappeared, hidden by muddy, forbidding clouds. The fields and trees and valley were suddenly colorless and drab, an ugly, lifeless gray that seemed to whisper ominously of impending death. Even though I knew I had done the right thing, there was an uneasiness in my heart.

"Lord," I prayed, "You have been leading me. I leave everything in Your hands."

The authorities did not wait long to act. Four detectives were waiting for me at the school when we got back.

And you shall even be brought [dragged] before governors and kings for My sake, as a testimony to them and to the Gentiles. But when they deliver you up, do not become anxious about how or what you will speak; for it shall be given you in that hour what you are to speak. For it is not you who speak, but it is the Spirit of your Father who speaks in you (Matthew 10:18–20 NASB).

As I repeated the tenth chapter of Matthew from memory, God opened a curtain on a little corner of the future. I knew that I was about to see the acts of the Lord, and joy drove away my nervousness and filled my heart.

"If you keep My commandments, you will abide in My love; just as I have kept My Father's commandments, and abide in His love" (John 15:10 NASB).

I thought I was being taken to the police station, but instead they took me to the office of the chief of the district. My fear of suffering was transformed into the thrill of starting some splendid adventure. My mind was calm. And why wouldn't it be? The Lord was sustaining me completely.

The detectives who brought me to the district chief bowed politely and left the room. He glanced at me and then directed his attention to his work once more. My breath almost stopped, for anger and hatred glittered in his eyes. His fierce, copper-colored face was a burning flame. All I could think of was that he must be an inspector from hell.

"Who do you think you are?" he demanded in Japanese. "Do you realize what you did at Namsan Mountain today? Why were you so reckless? Don't you know about our great imperial Japanese police power?" Our neighboring conquerors had ruled that all officials in the puppet government must speak Japanese while in their offices. The district chief tried to carry out the edict, but he spoke so brokenly that it was hard for me to keep from laughing. He caught the brief smile on my lips and surmised the reason.

"You miserable woman!" he exploded. "You think you are so smart! Do you want to see what we can do to you?"

"Do not fear!" the Lord told me. "The LORD will fight for you" (Exodus 14:13–14 NASB).

At that instant the phone rang. His entire manner changed. "Yes, sir. . . . Yes, sir. . . . Yes, sir." He sounded more like a machine than a man of position and authority. When the conversation was over, he seemed to have forgotten I was even in the room. Opening the cabinet behind his desk with trembling hands, he began to search frantically through the files. I realized God was fighting for me. He must have found what he was looking for because he put a paper into his bag and rushed out, leaving me alone.

Quickly I got to my feet and left, walking past the clerks in the outer office. With shaking legs, I ran out into the hall and walked out of the building as though nothing had happened. Outside, the sun was shining brightly and the blue of the sky reached far above the surrounding hills.

"O Lord," my heart was saying, "only You could do such a thing. I am in Your hands, Father. Help me to listen and obey You." I ran as I prayed. It didn't matter to me that the people on the street were watching me.

When I reached home the gate was locked, but Mother heard my frantic cry and ran barefoot to let me in. Several Christians were there praying for me. They were stunned when they saw me, but their astonishment gave way to gratitude and praise.

I was not in prison, but the danger was still present. "The Bible says that when they persecute you in one town," Mother advised me, "flee to the next. You must go as quickly as you can."

I knew that a description of me would soon be in the hands of every policeman on every street corner. I had to disguise myself, so I rubbed my face and hands with ashes and put on old-fashioned clothes and old rubber shoes of a country woman. While I was changing my appearance as much as possible, Mother wrapped up some clean clothes and my Bible in a cloth.

She didn't dare go with me; that would have been too dangerous for both of us. But she followed at a distance to see that I was able to get safely out of town. I reached the railway station just as a freight train was about to leave. I managed to board the lone passenger car on the end of the long freight only moments before it pulled out for Shin Ei Joo. The train was slow and would stop often, but all I was concerned about was leaving the city before being discovered by the police.

I sat down near the window and looked out at the gathering dusk. Now I knew how David must have felt when he was being chased by King Saul. He was like a small deer trying to get away from a powerful hunter. But God had known David's faith and watched over him, and later he was crowned king.

As the train groaned under the weight of its load, I leaned back in the hard, uncomfortable seat and closed my eyes. David must have wondered why he was persecuted, just as I wondered at what was happening to me. I could understand that David must have had to go through such suffering as part of the training for ruling the children of Israel with wisdom and compassion, but why was this happening to me? I had no answer. I was only an ordinary woman. No kingdom was awaiting my rule. Still, I knew that my Lord had ordered me to fight. I had no choice except to bear testimony of my Savior until I should die.

The train was one of those that stopped at every station. Each time it slowed down and came to a stop, I tensed and didn't relax until we began to move again and I was sure that no policemen had come aboard.

I began to wonder about the stars and planets that winked down at us so serenely. Was there any other planet like Earth where human beings lived? Would some of those people in the far reaches of the universe worship idols and persecute the disciples of the Lord? Is there heaven among the stars?

By dying I would go to heaven and see Jesus, together with the saints and martyrs who had died for Him. Jesus had come to this very small earth to save sinful human beings, giving His life for them on the cross.

The Japanese were crushing untold numbers of believers under their cruel, iron heel in Korea, but actually they had to stand powerless before the Lord. Just as the stars in the sky would not change, God's laws would not change. I wished to shine in the black night sky of my beloved country like a changeless star.

But, where am I going? What is going to happen to me? I thought.

When the train finally reached my chosen destination of Shin Ei Joo, my fears came rushing back. I retreated to the women's rest room and hid, shivering and shrinking in the unrelenting cold that held spring captive in that city just south of the Manchurian border. I was sandwiched between the ice of those dirty concrete walls that seemed oppressively close together. Finally I could stand the cold no longer and went out into the crowded waiting room where I found a corner and prayed that I would not be discovered.

I am one of those people who finds it difficult to withstand the discomfort of the cold. I did not believe I was afraid of death, but I dreaded facing my most dreadful enemy, the freezing cold of a concrete prison cell. The thought was crushing, and I wept in my heart as I told everything to the Lord. Just as an injured child finds comfort in her mother's sympathy, I prayed to Jesus, letting Him know the dejection that swept over me.

"It's so cold, Jesus," my heart whispered to Him. "Even my tears are like beads of ice on my cheeks, and I have no place to go."

I was still praying when I remembered that one of my former students was living in this same city. My heart leaped with joy, shaking itself free of sadness. I wanted to phone her at once, but I realized it would be best to wait until my young friend would be out of bed. I had never known time to creep by so slowly. It was an eternity before I felt that it was late enough for me to telephone her. Finding the number in the directory at the nearest public phone booth, I dialed it.

She came for me as quickly as she could, hurrying through the crowded streets. While I was waiting for her I changed my clothes in the rest room, washed my face and hands, and combed my hair. Kyung Shin found me, heard the reason for my unexpected visit, and called a taxi for the short ride to her parents' home.

She led me to a quiet room in a secluded part of the house which was warmed by an under-the-floor stove after the ancient *ondol* fashion. It was very comfortable. The room was Kyung's, I decided. I knew her well from school, and the furniture and ornaments showed her taste and hobbies.

"How is it with the Christians here?" I asked her.

"Persecution in the churches is severe," she said. The Christians who wanted to keep their faith had fled from the city.

"And what about yourself?"

The answer came quickly. She had stopped going to church, she said, but she kept her faith secretly.

A TEMPORARY HIDEOUT

Late that night I phoned my older sister. Mother had gone to the home of my sister and her husband at Jung Joo earlier in the day and was very concerned about me. It was decided that I, too, should go there. At the moment it was still quiet in the area where my sister lived, so I would be safer there. I knew I could not stay long with Kyung Shin because it would not be fair to her.

"I've heard there are no policemen on the last train," my sister told me. "If you hurry, I believe you can make it."

Although Kyung Shin was disappointed that I was leaving so soon, she understood.

I found a seat in an obscure corner of the train and hunched into it. It seemed to have been waiting in the station just for me. As soon as I was aboard the train, it began to move, gathering speed quickly in the dark night.

"This world is as dark as this night," I told myself. Everything on either side of the train was wrapped in shadows as black as an evil man's soul, but the sky was punctured with light as bright as ten thousand times ten thousand jewels gleaming with God's glory. *True faith should be like those stars,* I thought, *shining even brighter as the world becomes darker.*

I closed my eyes and began to pray.

When we got to the Jung Joo station, a messenger sent by my sister soon found me and took me over to where she was waiting for me in the darkness. She had brought their three German shepherd dogs with her. They were like so many faithful servants; she never went anywhere without them.

Although Jung Joo was still comparatively quiet, it had all the curiosity and loose tongues so characteristic of most small towns. My sister was extremely cautious lest my arrival would become known. That was a second reason for having me come late at night. Taking off her shawl, she put it on my shoulders. Then, with great care in order to walk as quietly as possible, we made our way through the sleeping town to her home.

The entire family was awake and waiting for us, but our first greeting was from the flock of geese she kept in the grassy area between her house and three factories which her husband owned and operated. They began to honk imperiously at the first sound of our footsteps, like dogs jealously guarding their master.

"That's enough," my sister ordered, and they quieted immediately. Seeing Mother, I wanted to cry for joy. I knew that her heart always was looking toward God. When we were alone at last, I told her all that had happened since I had been taken to the district director.

"I'm so thankful that God made you, who are a weak one, to act so quickly," she said joyfully. "It is indeed a miracle."

Praying with one mind that God would lead us according to His will, we left everything in His hands.

I was to learn later that the geese remained silent as the family came and went. Only when a stranger approached did they set up a clamor. Since there were usually visitors in the house, the geese protested their presence almost incessantly.

The German shepherd dogs walked about like well-trained guards. They were given certain food at a specific time and were trained to never eat anything else offered to them. They ate in order of their age, the oldest eating his food first while the other two waited. Then the second oldest ate. When they both had their fill, it was time for the youngest to eat.

Both the geese and the dogs knew their masters and served them, I observed. It helped me to realize clearly how I must faithfully serve my God who had created me and saved me. Mother, my sister, and I would faithfully serve God who had given the life of His only begotten Son to save us from sin and hell.

It was beautiful at my sister's, and I had plenty of time to read the Bible, but as one monotonous day followed another I began to feel uncomfortable about staying there.

My sister had her own family, and I wanted to be alone with Mother in a more quiet place. Even their expensive food was not the type which we enjoyed.

My sister understood our feelings, so it was decided that we would look for a house in a quiet area in the country and move there. Happily, my brother-in-law also agreed.

A PLACE
OF REFUGE

S pring had already blown its warm breath on the earth, carrying away the harshness of winter. All around us the world was painted in rainbow colors and caressed by the gentle rays of the warming sun. *If only spring would come to human hearts,* I thought as Mother and I went out to look for a house to rent. *If only the powers of Satan would soon be melted away like the snow.*

"Those that are not of the truth will pass away," my mother assured me when I shared my thoughts with her. "They look strong but they are only deceiving themselves and others."

"This is such an awful world and I am so weak."

"God shows His strength in the weak," she replied. "Those of us who are weak must rely on Him with all our hearts, and God loves us because of it."

I always felt strengthened when I talked with Mother about God and His love. I began to think that life might be worth living in this time of persecution. It might even be a truer picture of the believer to agonize, to suffer, to be hated and tortured, and even to be killed in obeying God's words rather than to live an ordinary, uneventful life.

Although my sister's house was located at the foot of the mountain some distance from town and the police office, there was always the chance that spies or the police would detect my presence. So, we decided to find a place in an entirely different area. As we walked, we came to a tiny straw-thatched house at the foot of a hill. It was in good repair, and the yard had been neatly swept.

"I don't believe anyone is living here," Mother ventured.

We soon discovered that she was right. No furniture was inside, but the place was clean and neat. There was a garden and in front of it a narrow crystal stream, murmuring happily to itself on its way to the river.

What had happened to this house? we wondered. *Who was the owner and why did he leave such a nice place with its beautiful rock fountain?*

We learned the story from a neighbor.

Tragedy had struck the elderly couple who lived there. First their son, who made his home with them, contracted tuberculosis and, after a long illness, died. Then the father died from the same disease, leaving the old woman alone. Because of the illness, no one came to visit her. She tried to sell the place, but people were afraid to live in it. Finally, unable to bear the loneliness, she loaded all that she owned on a cart and left. No one knew where she had gone, we were told, but they were sure she would never return.

Mother and I brought the matter before the Lord and were sure that this was to be my refuge. When we talked it over with my sister, however, she was strongly opposed, thinking that we, too, would contract the dreaded disease. I took her hands and told her that I was no longer a teacher.

"One day I will become a prisoner and will die in a cell somewhere. Do you think it is only two or three who have died from tuberculosis in jail? In this house I will prepare myself to go to that merciless jail."

Reluctantly my sister agreed, but she insisted on completely remodeling the house. Three men were sent from her husband's factories to break off all the dirt in the house and carry it away. They destroyed the floors completely, taking the refuse up the mountain a hundred or more meters. Then they dug new dirt from the mountain, bought new stones for the floor, and painted the walls. While they put new dirt on the outer walls, we washed the sliding screens with sterilizer and re-papered them.

Although we moved into the house without asking the owner's permission, we were determined to find her, if possible, and pay her liberally for the house.

The place turned out to be ideal for our purpose since no neighboring houses were nearby. I clothed myself like a country woman and was careful not to be conspicuous, but it was safe for me to sing praises to the Lord as loudly as I wanted and as often as I felt like it. During those days and weeks I sang and prayed and memorized more than one hundred chapters of the Bible as well as many hymns.

The sound of the stream was a lullaby, drawing me to its quiet bank and washing the strain from my mind. I planted a garden and got some potted flowers for the house. Never before had I worked with growing things. Living so simply was awakening in me a love for plants that I had never had before. The house was a refuge, built just for me, and I found a new strength arising from deep within my heart.

My sister visited us every evening, careful to avoid being noticed by the curious. She brought us fruit and other food, and we looked forward to each visit as a time when we could be together.

One evening an unfamiliar woman appeared in our neighborhood. As she walked slowly along the dusty road, an uneasy fear filled me for I suspected that she might be a spy. I soon learned differently. She was an evangelist who had quit going to church when a Japanese altar was placed there. She had fled to avoid arrest and was continuing to speak of the

Lord Jesus in faraway valleys and villages. I invited her in, and Mother and I talked with her around the table.

Mrs. Chang had not eaten much since leaving home, she told us. Because she had been visiting the poorer villagers who had little for her, she had to be content with only one meal a day. But due to the Lord's grace, she remained healthy and was still able to travel through the mountains.

"I wish you could have been with me on my travels," she said, her eyes glowing. "Even deep in the mountains I have heard believers praying. I have been in caves where pastors, evangelists, elders, and deacons were gathered together. Even though they were living off just the roots of mountain plants and water from the streams, they were strong and swift."

As I listened to her story, I thought of wicked Queen Jezebel and also of the dark age of Emperor Nero. It was almost as though God were flipping back the pages of countless calendars. When the woman looked at me, sorrow came to her eyes.

"You are like a princess, so frail and delicate," she said. "I wonder if you will be able to survive the hardship of persecution." She shook her head, almost as though she were doubting God's wisdom. "It's hard to understand why He would choose such a protected young lady to stand up for Him. But we shouldn't complain. We don't always know His will or purpose."

A few nights later someone knocked at our door. Since it was our practice to go to bed early in order to become accustomed to living without light, we had been asleep for hours and were surprised at this midnight visitor.

A kindly voice explained that our caller was Deacon Lee who had been told about us by Mrs. Chang. Getting up at once, Mother invited him in.

Although we had electricity, we only used a candle to chase away the gloom. Lights would have shouted to any chance passerby that there was something unusual going on at our house.

Our guest had a shaggy beard and was gaunt with hunger, but his eyes were clear and his face glowed with the joy of a true believer. He sat solemnly with us and prayed.

I had never before seen anyone devour his food as our visitor did. He kept eating one dish of food after another until everything my sister had brought us for the next day was gone. But we were happy to help him.

He had been in the mountains two years, he said, and had sent his family to relatives in Manchuria before he fled. During the summer he could live anywhere, for the trees grew thick and offered much protection. During the winter he would find a cave to keep him out of the snow and provide a little warmth.

Food was hard for him to find, but he had discovered that he could fast for a week without difficulty. He had spent as long as twenty days without food, eating snow for water.

"The cold bothers me the worst," he said quietly. "I have often fallen senseless from the cold."

Other believers like himself, who were hiding in the mountains, had memorized much of the Bible, so they were not afraid, no matter how much the Japanese might try to change the Bible.

When the time came for him to go, he thanked us deeply. "Let us endure until the end," he said as he left.

In spite of the fact that we had been extremely careful, my presence outside the village had not gone unnoticed. After Deacon Lee's visit, believers often came to our door. My sister brought a large amount of food for them.

Spring was at its peak, and the garden was growing rapidly. There was a certain mystery about it that made me amazed at God's love that had caused Him to create.

When the rains came, which was often at that time of year, I would open all the windows so I could hear the muted symphony of wind and rain and the sharp staccato of thunder. Lightning flashed in the dark heavens, laying bare the mountains and valleys to my eyes. I marveled at the great display.

The universe was declaring that all things had remained the same since the day of creation.

Why did human beings change while nature remained unchanged? Why did man alone rebel against God, the Creator, while all other things remained as beautiful and pure as they were at the time of creation? At times unfamiliar melancholy took hold of me.

The sky in early summer was refreshing. The rains slacked off, but cotton clouds still lingered over the mountains. Restlessly and in ever-changing patterns, they crept across the sky, free from any laws or regulations. They were completely free. How wonderfully clouds had been used in the holy works of God! When the Israelites were led by Moses to leave Egypt, there was "a pillar of cloud by day to lead them on the way, and . . . a pillar of fire by night to give them light" (Exodus 13:21 NASB), and in order to hide God's people from the enemy. The clouds had never rebelled against their Creator.

I went often to the stream in front of the garden, and when the water was low I discovered so many tiny grasses and weeds and flowers, each with its unique beauty, that I marveled at the infinite variety to be found in God's creation. I whispered to Jesus, "I am like these nameless plants, a hidden, frail flower nobody knows. But like these plants, help me grow so that I can blossom and offer my faith, which You have given me, to others."

5

PREPARING
FOR PERSECUTION

Reports coming from the continuing stream of midnight
visitors were increasingly disturbing. As the fires of war
burned brightly, the Japanese were jerking young men
from every household, forcing them to the battlefields. Complaining parents were dragged off to jail charged with traitor-
ous thoughts. Women and children lived in constant fear that
their husbands and fathers might be taken next.

Increasing military activity brought a corresponding increase in forced worship at the Japanese shrines that were
springing up everywhere. Every pupil from kindergarten
through high school was forced to buy a charm of the Japanese
shrine and take it home.

"You are to paste it in the most important room in the
house," they were told, "and worship it morning and evening."

Our Christian visitors spoke in awe and horror of the terrible torture which faithful pastors were going through for
their faith. They were hung upside down while boiling water
mixed with hot peppers was forced through their noses into
their stomachs. When their bellies would hold no more, they

were dropped on their heads on the cement floor, to be kicked and walked on by their tormentors. And when the water had come out of their nostrils, mouths, and rectums, the ugly process was repeated.

Men were whipped until the leather lashes ripped skin and flesh and broke bones. Hands were placed on wooden boards and whipped until they became useless masses of flesh. Bamboo needles were forced beneath finger and toenails, causing pain that cannot even be imagined, and glass bottles were used as clubs until they broke, slashing faces and skulls, and driving bloody slivers of glass deep into features that no longer looked human.

"In the end they go mad," our informants whispered. "Terrible things go on behind the bars."

I felt faint to think of what would happen to me. "How long will I be able to endure?" I kept asking myself.

I knew it would be impossible for me to keep my faith in my own power. God would have to work through me if I was to stand firm. I decided to fast.

Many times I had fasted for three days without difficulty. Now, however, I was determined to go without food and drink while I prayed for a week. After three days I had trouble breathing. On the sixth and seventh days, my lips were dry and my chest was in an iron vise, causing me to fight to breathe. Everything around me was blurred and dim, and my nerves were as taut and twisted as so many strands of rope. When the fast was over and my mother put water into my mouth, I raised my voice in victory, thanking God for being with me.

Although I had not expected it, after the fast I was able to understand the Scriptures better and I felt a new power in my prayer. Now I felt that I could leave the fear of torture in the Lord's hands.

But it was not to be so easily accomplished.

As even more fearful news came to me, I became anxious

again. "This time," I told Mother, "I'm going to fast for ten days."

Those ten days were ten months to me. The color of my eyes changed, and my breath became so offensive that nobody would come near me. My blood circulation was so low and weak that I was sure that, this time, I would die. I am quite sure that I was very close to death.

"O Lord," I kept telling Him, "this is so much better than torture."

My mother and sister suffered more than I. When the fast was over, they were both so exhausted and concerned for me that they were ill. But when the tenth day finally ended, how I thanked the Lord. I was as happy as though I had conquered the world.

Again I found a peace I had never known before. I read the Bible earnestly and had a new concern to memorize important chapters against the day when I would be in prison without my Bible.

On one occasion I awoke before dawn and, as I read my Bible by candlelight, I developed a severe headache. Never having had a headache before, I was annoyed. The medicine Mother gave me for it had little effect.

"Is this what the pain will be like if I'm hit on the head by the policemen?" I asked her. "I can hardly stand it."

"Let's talk to Jesus and ask Him to heal it."

We all prayed about my headache, but it continued without easing in intensity. The third day after we started praying, an elderly, kindly woman evangelist, wearing a snow white robe, came into my room quietly not long before dawn. Even now I don't know if it was a dream or a vision. Approaching me, she sat down and gently tapped my forehead several times. I woke up and looked around, but there was no such woman in the room. Only my mother was there, kneeling near me, praying. I was free from the headache, and my heart was greatly uplifted.

Wouldn't Jesus, who healed the terrible pain in my head,

do the same when I was tortured? *He may not even allow the Japanese to torture me,* I thought. Like my fasting experiences, the headache helped me to have strength and hope.

When I shared my experience with the other believers who had come down from the mountains and the caves, they told me how the Lord had been helping them, almost daily, in the same miraculous way. For the first time in my life, I wished I were a man so I could also hide in a mountain or a cave, drinking the dew and snow, and eating roots of grass and the bark of trees, and finally dying there.

6

NOWHERE
TO LAY MY HEAD

Both Mother and I knew that the peaceful, happy life we were experiencing in the straw-thatched house would not last long, but we were unprepared for its sudden collapse. The sun had set and darkness was creeping in from the mountains one evening when my sister hurried into the house. Even as we saw her rushing up the road, we knew that something had gone wrong.

"The Japanese know you are around here," she told me, her voice shrill with fear. "A policeman came to the house and asked a maid where you were. I could hear them from a back room!"

I would be safe for the night, we decided. It was unlikely that my hiding place would be discovered so quickly, but I had to flee early the next morning. My sister decided she would go with me.

Again I dressed in the simple manner of the country people. I combed my hair the way a farm girl would, wore rubber shoes, and wrapped my Bible and a change of clothes in an old handkerchief. I was anxious—even frightened—but an adventurous excitement overtook me.

Although my legs were not strong, I was prepared to go as far as I could. I would firmly trust in the Lord's promises and would rely on Him. Whatever might happen, I would follow His will cheerfully.

In the half-light of early dawn, my sister, who also had dressed herself as simply as possible, and I said good-bye to Mother and left. We could have taken a bus or train from the nearby town to our chosen destination, but we decided that would be too dangerous. Since the police knew I was in the area, the risk was too great for us to go into the town, even so early in the morning.

It was hard for Mother to see me leave. She followed behind us and stopped at the corner to watch until we disappeared from sight. My heart bled to see her there, looking so sad and beautiful. But we could not stop, because we had to get as much distance between us and the searching policemen as possible.

As we made our way over the narrow mountain paths, the sun, climbing higher in the vaulted, cloudless sky, glistened brighter on the endless green of the valley that stretched behind us. Though we were far from the sea, a song of sailing sprang from my heart.

> Launch out into the deep, Oh, let the shoreline go:
> Launch out, launch out in the ocean divine,
> Out where the full tides flow.
> People stand on shore, look at the waves
> But do not try to see how deep the sea is.
> Now lift anchor and sail to the ocean of grace:
> Sail to that fathomless ocean of Jesus Christ's love.

I sang as we walked, and my sister joined me. I knew I might not be able to cross all the high mountains of persecution that lay ahead of me, and the tears flowed as I thought of Mother, who was left alone now with her aching heart. She would be even more dependent upon the Lord than before.

At last we came to a village where we could take a bus to Ku Sung, the city where my sister's son lived with his family. Apprehension gripped us as we realized that we would have to expose ourselves to the stares of strangers and to the risk of being discovered by an alert policeman. Then I remembered that we had walked many kilometers over stony mountain paths. My feet weren't blistered in spite of the fact that I was wearing hot, ill-fitting rubber shoes. Neither were we tired.

"God is working a miracle," I whispered with assurance to my sister. "We have nothing to fear."

Confidently we rode the bus to Ku Sung. On the way from the bus stop to my nephew's home, I combed my hair and wiped as much of the dirt from my face as possible. My sister's son was a well-known surgeon and owned a large hospital, which was attached to the house. She explained my situation to him and his wife and asked if I could stay with him for a while. They offered me their quietest room.

My sister took the first bus back to her home the following day.

I had never realized how noisy a hospital could be. A dam was being built across the nearby Amnokang River, and with tens of thousands of workers, there were many injuries. The first night I was awakened several times by the groaning of patients. The next morning the groans and screams increased tenfold.

I couldn't stay calm. For some reason I was acutely sensitive to such cries of suffering. My nerves were raw, and I felt as though the pain of the injured would penetrate my body.

"This is what torture will be like," I told myself. I felt as though hell itself had taken up residence in that home. Everyone else was at ease; I was the only one who was restless and trembling. I was ashamed of myself.

My nephew and his wife were kind to me. Not realizing the agony I was experiencing, they invited me to stay until the end of the summer. As if I were in prison, I told myself to be patient. I thought I would get used to it, but, instead, I became even more distressed. By the end of the week I had lost my appetite and was unable to sleep. Finally I realized that I could endure it no longer. I didn't know where I would go, but this much I knew: I had to leave.

A short bus ride away, I found a little mountain hotel where I stayed for a night. But even as I took a room, I realized it would not provide a safe haven because there were too many people around. I went even farther back in the mountains to a remote village where few passengers got off. I paid my fare and followed them.

Once more I changed clothes and combed my hair in the country style. I didn't know what I was going to do or where I was going or even where I was. Leaving the bus stop, I went into the section of the village where the homes of the people were located. Children clustered curiously around me. Embarrassed and fearful, I asked them to take me to the church.

The door was not locked, so I went inside. Even here in this remote place a shrine had been placed high in the center of the altar. Dismayed, I ran out of the church and went back to the mountain.

Although I felt rejected by everyone, the mountain with its grass and trees welcomed me. All of nature seemed to whisper words of encouragement to me that morning. Yet, I was still not at rest. I sat on a large boulder and opened my Bible. God was there, speaking to me.

> But we have this treasure in earthen vessels, that the surpassing greatness of the power may be of God and not from ourselves; we are afflicted in every way, but not crushed; perplexed, but not despairing; persecuted, but not forsaken; struck down, but not destroyed; always carrying about in the body the dying of Jesus, that the life of Jesus also may be manifested in our body (2 Corinthians 4:7–10 NASB).

As I read, I began to understand that I was now becoming a *true* believer. I was also in affliction. I resolved that I must die a death that would befit a Christian, as Jesus Himself and many of His faithful followers had. The ice of anxiety in the bottom of my heart melted away.

"Glory be unto thee, O my soul!"

Without noticing what I was doing, I began to sing cheerfully. I got to my feet and walked along the path, singing as I went. Snowy clouds were glistening in the sun as they glided busily about the sky.

It was clouds just like those that, in old times, had led the Israelites. They also promised to play a wonderful role at the time of Jesus' return.

My joy seemed to become frost as I saw men in the mountain cutting firewood. Somewhere men were searching for me. Sometime they would find me; that I knew. I climbed a tall pine tree, looked up at the clouds, and my heart was sore for my mother. My sister would care for her, yet I knew she would be tossing sleeplessly on her bed, consumed by concern for me. It was toward evening and I had no idea where I should sleep. "Foxes have holes," Jesus had said, "and the birds of the air have nests; but the Son of Man has nowhere to lay His head" (Matthew 8:20 NASB).

Somewhere within the inner reaches of my mind I had a slight complaint. Jesus' situation must have been a little better than mine, I decided, for He was a man.

As darkness came, I could see the lights of a small village. I walked in that direction, wondering what I would find. I knew that in most cases families and neighbors would be gathering outside, fanning away the mosquitoes as they talked endlessly. I kept walking along the dark path, avoiding the places where people would be apt to see me. Finally I found a farmhouse, set apart from the other houses and some distance from the village.

"Excuse me," I said, approaching some people in the yard. A woman's voice in a strong country accent asked what I wanted.

"Would you please let me stay with you one night?"

Silence greeted me, and sadness arose in my heart. "May I come in?" I asked, stepping into the yard.

"Who are you?" an old man asked in a hoarse voice.

I told him I was a traveler and could walk no longer. I repeated my request to stay with them for the night. I was shocked at my boldness, but I walked toward the room from which I had heard the woman's voice. "Excuse me, ma'am," I said, "could I stay here for one night?"

"Yes," she told me.

Some offensive smell caused me to be nauseated as I entered the room, but there was no time for me to be disturbed by it. Dirtiness or bad smells could not bother me now. I held my nose with my fingers, and lay down.

When I awakened in the morning, I found that the household was quite poor. There seemed to be no expression at all on the wife's face as she prepared breakfast, and the three-year-old girl had the same dull unhappiness about her. It was as though she had willed herself to feel nothing, not even the nagging malnutrition and hunger that distended her little stomach and made her eyes protrude. She was completely lacking in beauty.

The wife went out to work, and since I couldn't remain there alone with the old man, I had to leave the house. I patted the girl on the head and made a funny face, but she did not respond.

On my way up the mountain, I thought about her. Although she did not know laughter and obviously had nothing in her life that was good or pleasing, she was free. Her possession of freedom could have caused her to be far happier than I. Freedom had more value than clothes or food or knowledge or high position. But, at the same time, that vacant young face lacked true freedom. What had Jesus said? "The truth shall make you free" (John 8:32). Without this truth there could be no real freedom. That was why I had to fight my battle through to the end. I had to keep this freedom given by Jesus.

I looked up at the mountain, knowing that one mountain

stood behind another as far as I could see or think. My future was like those endless mountains. I felt that I would never be able to cross them all.

I saw farmers working in the field, but I was careful not to get close enough for them to pay attention to me. It was comparatively easy for me to avoid the men who were tilling their crops, but I dreaded going over the mountains. The paths were narrow and the hills were so steep that there was no way for me to go around those men who were cutting wood, even on the highest mountain. Few women walked alone in such remote areas, so the men would be curious if they saw me.

I began to resent the fact that I was a woman. If I were only a man, I thought, I could sing a hymn as I walked. Then, I reasoned, it would not be long until other believers would hear me and would come out of the forest singing the same hymn. Thus I would have friends and fellowship. But I was a woman; I dared not do such a thing. Resting wearily under a tree, I looked at myself for the first time since I had left my nephew's home. My wrinkled summer clothes had not been washed for days, and I looked as sad and as miserable as I felt.

Suddenly an amusing thought made me laugh until I tumbled off the big stone I was sitting on. I had been an actor in a marvelous play on the great stage of the earth, the same play in which those martyrs had been who had fought and died to defend the truth. At that moment it seemed that they were looking down at me somewhere behind those clouds.

"Be courageous," I told myself.

As I said those two words, self-pity fled and I was able to continue cheerfully on, reciting Bible verses or singing hymns in rhythm to my pace.

Looking up into the heavens, I prayed to Jesus with every step, leaning on Him and asking Him to give me strength. And, though I walked continuously in the strong summer sun, my feet did not ache nor did I become thirsty. Again I was filled with happiness.

My situation was the same as when the Israelites were led

out of Egypt. Great joy filled my heart and overflowed to the heavens and the earth.

"I shall die," I told myself quietly. "At this time I shall die, just as Christians in former times died for the sake of the truth." Unable to find words of thanksgiving suitable for this wonderful honor, I just kept crying. At the same time I felt a great burden in my heart. I knew, or thought I knew, what a hard road I would have to walk before death came.

At last it was evening and I was in a fairly large village. I was looking for a rice-cake shop where I could buy some food and sit for a few minutes to rest. Such a place would be safe, I thought. They didn't sell alcohol or cigarettes as was done in restaurants, so spies or detectives were unlikely to come there. And rice-cake shops were usually owned by the poor who would have more compassion than the wealthy.

"Would you have a room where I can stay tonight?" I asked the owner of the shop where I made my purchase.

She showed me a room, and I lay down on the floor, using my bundle as my pillow. I was so weary I went to sleep nearly at once, but not for long. Almost immediately I was awakened by someone kicking me. I opened my eyes and looked around, but no one was there. Then I realized that the Holy Spirit had jarred me out of my sleep. Evidently it was not safe for me to remain in that place, so as quietly as possible, I slipped out of the house and left the village. All night I walked, guided by the bright light of the stars and the moon.

I was not at all sleepy until just before dawn, when the skies became black and impenetrable and the cold increased in intensity. I sat down then, the darkness and shivering cold wrapping me in loneliness. As soon as it was light, I got to my feet and started on, fighting against the cold and my lack of sleep.

I looked like a country peddler with a bundle of wares, I thought. To me that was comical. When I came to a rather large town across the mountain, I walked about like a woman peddler. No one paid any attention to me. Seeing that the primary school had a large playground, my heart leaped. I decided that the playground's center was going to be my bedroom for the night.

I ascended the mountain near the town until nighttime when the children were at home. My heart was at ease as I knelt on the hard ground in the center of the playground and buried my face in my bundle as if to greet my heavenly Father on a special occasion. But my tears flowed until my bundle became soaking wet and I could only cry out, "O Lord, heavenly Father!"

Apparently I fell asleep, for suddenly I heard a gentle, familiar voice saying, "Go to Pyongyang."

I woke up and looked around. Again, nobody was there. The moon had disappeared, and the playground was veiled in darkness.

Great strength and happiness sprang from deep within my heart. I had heard the Lord's voice!

Tying up my bundle again, I stood up and walked toward town. I had to go out into the main street where the buses stopped. I knew my stomach would not growl in hunger since I would not be able to wait until the rice-cake shops opened to get food, for it had been trained from many times of fasting. I would not even have time to get anything to drink.

I was following the leading of the Lord! I was on my way to Pyongyang.

7

"GO TO PYONGYANG"

I went confidently to the main street to wait for the bus. Having heard the voice of God telling me to go to Pyongyang, I knew He was directing me. I would listen to Him and follow His leading. Wasn't He, the Creator of the universe, my Father? I had no need to worry when I could hold the hands of Jesus and remember His words of promise until the moment I entered heaven. Within my heart I could hear the "Hallelujah Chorus" played by a powerful and radiant orchestra. My tears shrouded the entire world in mist, making it more like a dream than reality.

When the bus for Shinijoo came, I got on it in obedience to the Lord's command. I was somewhat fearful because I was known in Shinijoo, but no one on the bus seemed to recognize me. As soon as we reached the city, I hurried into the station, changed clothes, and washed my face and combed my hair. Country women seldom ventured so far from their villages, and I wasn't eager to attract attention.

I waited for the nightly passenger-freight train, making myself as inconspicuous as possible in a corner of the plaza. It was noon the next day when the slow-moving train reached Pyongyang. A crowd in the distance was shouting, *"Banzai! Banzai!"* to the discordant clamor of the drums. Cautiously, I walked toward them.

An express train loaded with young Japanese soldiers had just arrived from Japan and was going on to the battlefield. Everyone was at the station: the leading officials, policemen, students, and ordinary citizens. Japanese flags were waving while the people shouted, *"Banzai,"* and the students in uniform were singing a patriotic number, accompanied by the band.

I was not listening to the din around me. My gaze was fixed on the solemn, expressionless faces of the young servicemen. They looked like so many corpses headed for unmarked graves on the battlefields of China, living sacrifices to the gods of imperialism and military might. Numbly I walked alongside the train, fighting for each breath. The soldiers all had that strange look of death, as though they were being sent to hell for the sake of the state.

Didn't the Bible say that the wages of idolatry were wars, famines, and pestilences? Because of it, youth would die in wars, young wives would become widows, parents would lose their sons, children would become orphans, and peace would vanish. Idolatry would cause all the world to be visited with calamities. Leaders of the state were responsible, for they were committing sins and sowing the seeds of curse.

Someone had to take the Gospel to those young men who were condemned to an early death. Someone had to seek out each one and tell him the Good News from God that Jesus Christ had come to save him. Someone must save these tens of thousands of fine young men from the road to hell.

I stomped the ground and cried in my frustration and anger. If only someone in a high position would stand up to the Japanese leaders and make them see that the youth from all over the country were turning into fiends in hell, day after day. There was no time to waste. It had to be done quickly.

That burden tormented me like a fire that would not be quenched. Then, suddenly I heard a voice speaking to my heart. "You are one! You must do it!"

I straightened in surprise. That couldn't be! I was only a woman without strength or wisdom. I was a weakling, a child of sin. Yet, my burning heart became as peaceful as a glassy sea.

"Listen to the Lord," I told myself. I still couldn't quite believe it, and I felt an urge to cry, but a hymn resounded in my innermost being: "Glory to Thee." The words kindled a new excitement in me as I went out of the railway station.

8

A FOREBODING
OF TERROR

I had graduated from an exclusive girls' school in Pyong-yang, so I knew the city quite well. I walked confidently along the busy streets with the same rushed preoccupation that seemed to rule everyone else. No one was paying any attention to me, a fact I liked.

I already had decided I would visit my niece, who was attending another girls' school in the city. She would surely have word from home, I thought. When she saw me, she came running out and whispered, "Mother has left our house and is here with me. And, of course, Grandmother is with us, too."

"Thank You, Lord!" my heart sang. "Thank you! Thank you!"

My mother and sister told me how detectives and policemen had come to the house after I left and repeatedly asked about me. Finally, the pressure had become so great that Mother and my sister felt it was best for them to leave.

"Christians from all over this part of Korea have come here to Pyongyang," they said. "They have changed their occupations and are living in secret."

I told Mother what I had seen and heard at the railway station.

Her reaction was startling to me.

"The time has come for you to prepare yourself to die," she said.

Death was coming for me! By this time all three of us were aware of it. I had to prepare myself for imprisonment; I had to practice to die.

The first step was to learn to live in deep poverty. Mother and I rented a house near the open market and moved in. People were everywhere, and it became our daily routine to go out to the market with tracts when we weren't praying or worshiping God or memorizing Bible verses. Everyone was in such a hurry that it was difficult to talk to them about our Savior. All we could do was hand out tracts. "Let us believe in Jesus," we would say. "Please read this."

At first we were bashful and awkward and found it difficult, but eventually it became enjoyable. Most of the people were polite and would bow their heads in gratitude. "Thank you very much," they would say. "I will certainly read this literature."

Others grimaced scornfully, and ridicule sharpened their voices. When that happened, I would run after them and say, "Give it back to me." I couldn't stand to see a tract that could bring some soul to Christ go to waste on an unrepentant, disinterested heart.

I think my sister must have been embarrassed many times by my actions. "That is your way, isn't it?" she would ask.

But my mother scolded her gently. "You can't say you are truly dead unless you destroy that nature, can you?" she asked.

Her words touched my heart. I did not speak aloud, but my thoughts were sad. *Only with my mouth do I talk of dying,* I realized.

I had grown up in a home where I had been made to believe that it was a lowly thing for an intelligent young woman with a good education to visit the open market. That was for the peasants and the laborers who lacked the money to buy elsewhere. I had not known much about markets, but I discovered that many of the merchants were women who had only flawed goods to sell. They offered overripe, half-rotten fruits and vegetables, or food too dry to be sold at any other place.

"These are cheap and good!" they would shout all day long in a frantic effort to get customers. "Cheap! Cheap! Extremely cheap!"

After crying out continually, their voices were hoarse, but still there were few customers. Those who did want to buy would haggle over the price until tempers raged and the quarreling was bitter. The eyes of the market vendors were tired and dull, and the stench of unwashed bodies and rotting food was in their clothes. Although they were women, their voices were as coarse and harsh as men's.

I would visit those poor, unhappy merchants, often buying their remaining goods at the same price I would pay for unspoiled food. I witnessed to them, and they listened to me.

My actions would have seemed extremely strange to anyone who may have been watching me. Every day I went over the food I had bought, sorting out the decaying vegetables and fruits, the dried rice cakes, and those things most people would have considered unfit to eat. Those I saved for myself. The rest I gave to my mother, who ate very little, and to the neighbors.

Tears moistened Mother's eyes as she watched me, but she quickly understood. In prison I knew they would serve me rotten beans and millet, so that is what I bought and ate. At first my sister cried when she saw the food I had selected for myself. Gradually, however, she, too, came to see the reason for my actions.

Until then I only could believe in faith that God had sent me to Pyongyang. The time was soon coming, however, when I would see the proof of it. As time went by, we found many Christians who disguised themselves, used secret names, and hid in secret places all over the city in order to flee from the Japanese police.

Once, late at night, my sister brought one of these Christians to our home. Looking at me, he remarked, "It is a miracle that a believer like you, ma'am, who has been educated solely by the Japanese, has joined this line of martyrdom."

I felt so embarrassed about being spoken of in such a manner that I could not raise my head. He told about countless numbers of devout Christians, both by themselves and with their families, who had fled to Pyongyang on all the roads from the south, and even from Manchuria and China. They had come because they refused to take part in the shrine worship the Japanese were forcing upon us.

He named them, believers who reminded me of the persecution in the early Christian era. Like those believers of another day, they shared their belongings and helped each other. Regardless of their own status in life, they made themselves lowly and poor. They had such a spirit of generosity that they shared even little things, strengthening each other, and sacrificing themselves, if necessary, so that others might live.

We decided to meet at the house of Teacher Kim. When he first came to Pyongyang with his family, it had been difficult for him to find a house. About that same time the missionaries of Pyongyang Seminary had been sent back to America by the Japanese because they refused to worship at the Japanese shrine. The students had been scattered, leaving the school buildings unoccupied. Teacher Kim moved secretly into the school's empty guardhouse.

The house was well suited for our meeting. Situated away from the central part of the city, it was in an area of few buildings, and it was large enough for us to meet there. We took great care to go to the house late every Friday night, gathering quietly and without talking. The risk for such a meeting was great. Still, we met quietly, sang hymns in low voices, read the Bible, gave testimonies, and prayed. Our prayers were long and serious. Just before dawn we left the house in ones and twos, finding our ways through the darkened streets to our own homes.

We fasted as a group and made it a habit to eat as plainly as possible and to sleep without using quilts. Although we were all poor, we were never in want, and our houses and clothes were clean. We were all filled with the Holy Spirit and were convinced it was more than an honor to die for the Lord. We constantly lived in fear of the police, but we were happy and satisfied, envying no one. Having prayed all night, Pastor Power Chae would often stand up in joy, dancing and singing, while tears ran down his cheeks.

For us, it was a joyous blessing to have been born in such a place and for such a time. I realized that it was because of this persecution that I was able to truly experience God's presence and trust His promises.

At this time the police department released Reverend Joo and a few other pastors who had been imprisoned and tortured dreadfully. Believers flocked around them to comfort them and to gain strength from the strength which God had given to them. My sister and I, wrapped in mufflers to avoid being discovered, went to see Reverend Lee, a young pastor who had been in the group. We were all sure that one day we, too, would be imprisoned, so we wanted to learn what it would be like.

Pastor Lee was young in years, but the persecution had aged his body. His face was pale and colorless, and his tall frame was gaunt and weak with starvation. The calm account of his prison experiences only intensified our anguish.

"Doesn't a miracle happen during such torture, dear Pastor?" someone asked, voicing the question which I wanted answered most.

He closed his eyes for a long while, and we waited for an answer. "No miracle was worked in my case," he said, his voice growing weak as though he were reliving the months of torture again. "Actually, I was expecting one. I was waiting for God to intervene and save me from the devil whip that bit into my flesh and tore at my bones. But there was no such miracle. The pain and suffering were so great that I was about to curse my being alive. I couldn't understand why this life didn't come to an end. I wondered if God had forsaken me, and I regretted that I did not die."

Sighs of tension and horror escaped our lips. I felt as though someone had covered my eyes with a black cloth from which there was no escape.

I asked my sister to take me to Reverend Joo's home so I could hear him tell of his experiences. We went at midnight so there would be less chance that the authorities would be watching his house.

Sitting on a chair, Reverend Joo was dressed in white Korean clothes. The room was packed with believers sitting on the floor squeezed as close together as possible. Somehow they found room for all of us.

"The cruel whip tears the flesh," he said as casually as though he were describing a walk in the park. "My nerves felt as though they were being burned by fire. The only way of escaping was to faint. I have no idea how much torture is awaiting us, but do not expect a miracle to spare you. Men killed Christ on the cross in the same way."

I was struck dumb, as though I had been clubbed. I cried until I thought I could cry no more, and I was not alone. Every face in that room was as wet as mine.

The following Sunday morning Reverend Joo returned to the pulpit of Sundung Jae Presbyterian Church. The news spread rapidly, and believers congregated at the building in great numbers. Although I hurried to the church two hours before the service was to begin, more than 2,000 persons already were jammed into the large building. And still people came, moving silently into the church and standing along the walls at the rear and sides. At last I found a tiny niche where I could sit down.

Already my heart was heated with a holy flame. While waiting, I closed my eyes and prayed silently. Someone whispered that there were scores of detectives in the audience, but that fact bothered none of us. Reverend Joo sat alone on the platform. To me, he looked like a portrait of Jesus, for there was such an air of holiness about him. A power seemed to go out from him that would have soothed any angry man. I shall never forget that service or the hymn by Robert Grant that started it:

> O worship the King all glorious above,
> O gratefully sing His pow'r and His love;
> Our Shield and Defender, the Ancient of Days,
> Pavilioned in splendor and girded with praise.

The message that morning was on the theme of martyrdom. Using the Bible to explain his meaning, Reverend Joo told how dangerous it was to violate the law of God with human or state power. He talked of the leprosy that broke out on the face of King Uzziah when he violated the Lord's law, and then he related that incident to his own experience. All the people in the congregation were filled with the Holy Spirit as they heard the message.

I became even more determined that I would go forth as a chosen soldier of God to drive away the devils from this earth. With God's help I would not violate His law.

After the service I looked out at the distant horizon. Suddenly I stopped where I was. I felt that I saw a cross far beyond the hill. And that was my way. I had to go toward it.

I would be hated, despised, and cast aside. I, too, would be hanged on the cross. If this was the only way of truth and obedience to God's law, I would dash boldly toward it.

What was life? It could be beautiful if it were righteous, whether it was long or short; but it was the same as that of an animal if it was lived against God's law. While young and pretty and fresh and bold, I would give my life to God honorably and without reservation. I would keep the truth to the end. I would die telling others of the love of our blessed Lord.

My goal was death!

9

THE ELIJAH
OF THIS DAY

An old stranger came to our house one morning when we were at the breakfast table. Through the window we could see that he was in tattered Korean clothes and held a stick in his hand.

"Is Miss Ahn in this house?" he called out. He entered in response to our invitation. "Oh thank You, Lord!" he said prayerfully. "I've finally found her."

He told us he was Elder Park and that he had come looking for me because he had heard God tell him to go to Pyongyang to see Miss Ahn.

Joining us at breakfast, he told us his story. After being trained as a young man in Chinese medicine, he had treated many patients. But one day he gave the wrong injection to a child, and the boy died immediately. Placing the boy on the floor, he began to pray.

"Lord, revive this child. Work the same miracle as You did in Bible times, and I shall follow and obey You as Your faithful servant."

Without any sleep or food, he prayed for three days. Then

the child came back to life, he said, and is still living to this day. And, since Japan had begun to persecute believers, God had repeatedly talked to him.

"I have been a Christian for over fifty years," he continued. "But I have never heard God's voice so clearly as in these days. When the world is at peace, not very many people diligently seek God. Only at such times as these of persecution and disorder by the hands of Satan do believers awaken in faith."

One day he had been dragged into the police office, where he was ordered to worship the shrine. When he refused, he was struck and kicked brutally. Since he was an old man, he was released for a while. This was when God had him come to find me.

"The time has come to choose selected soldiers of Christ," the voice said. "Go to Pyongyang and meet Miss Ahn."

Upon hearing the voice, he obeyed, with God leading him. When he reached our house, he knew that was where I lived. He talked quite differently from most Koreans. His small physique, his tiny eyes and nose and wrinkled face were filled with courage, as if to testify to the truth of his story. Seeing the doubt in our faces, he was disturbed.

"Can't you see?" he asked impatiently. "What would happen if God kept silent at such a time as this when Satan is working so powerfully to kill men spiritually? It is at such a time as this that God works even more zealously to protect His believers. It is at such a time when God never rests."

I knew he was speaking the truth, for God had spoken to me as well. "Go to Pyongyang," He said.

I remembered all those Japanese soldiers at Pyongyang station being sent out to the battlefield, how I was shocked that they all looked like they were dead, and how I cried out that they would all die and go into eternal death unless someone brought the Gospel to them. I realized that their leaders were to blame. It was then that I heard a voice in my heart saying, "You must do it!"

"What did God tell you to do when you met me?" I asked him.

"God wants to warn the Japanese. You are an excellent speaker in their language, but when I first saw you I knew that you are weak in your faith. Yes, you are weak physically and also a weak believer. In fact, you still do not believe me."

I was indignant and hurt, but I had to admit that his words were true. Staggered, I asked him, "And so?"

"I want to walk before you," he told me, "and show you what faith is and how a believer should die for his God."

I was interested in what he said. "You are going to show me how to die for our Lord?"

"I fear nothing." A holy fire burned in his eyes. "I bear the task of Elijah. Everyone is so afraid that no one warns Japan. I have already been chosen by His holy voice. You have been chosen, too, haven't you? In that I am not mistaken."

I was like the others. Fear stopped my tongue.

"You speak Japanese, don't you?" he persisted.

"Yes."

"That is what we need: your good Japanese. But I have come to understand that you are a beautiful believer. What good can your excellent language do without faith? God has led me here so that He can use you. I am about to shout for joy, just as a horse that can run a thousand miles makes a joyful noise seeing another that can run ten thousand miles." Digging his bony fingers into his beard and twisting it thoughtfully, he said, "You are afraid of the torture, aren't you?"

I confessed that I was very much afraid.

"You need not be. God will surely hide us and blind their eyes. The Bible is the promise of power of the living God. What does it say? God is my refuge. God will hide us from enemies."

"Can that be possible?" my doubting heart asked him. I blushed as I realized I had voiced my unbelief.

"Can you say such faith is true faith?" he demanded.

I was saddened by his question.

This old man brought a quiet change to me. I had been trying like a fanatic to obtain a solution simply by fasting for the persecution which I knew was coming to me. What an honorable privilege it would be if such a worthless one as I would be able to die for the Lord! Now I felt the time had come.

Would the Japanese kill us instantly in the way which the Romans had executed their prisoners? Or would they leave us for ten or even twenty years in prison, starving, freezing, afflicted, and suffering? I feared that the most.

The difference between this old man and the other believers I knew was that he was dashing toward death while we were waiting for it.

Late at night I took him to the underground church and introduced him. He told the people the same story which he had told me. The people listened to him eagerly; but because of his extreme faith and frank words, some seemed to be offended. At the most, only half of them even believed him, but a few of the Christians rejoiced. Thus, he became a member of our group.

My heart became a battleground. The people came to believe that my task was the same as Elder Park's, that God had chosen the two of us to warn Japan. I found excuses for myself. Elder Park was a brave soldier of Christ who could fearlessly warn the Japanese government, but I was merely a woman, and besides, I was afraid. I would not be responsible for this task. I even found this verse of Scripture to lean upon: "Let woman learn in a quietness with all subjection" (1 Timothy 2:11).

So it was that I sought peace within my heart. During the daylight hours, I could make myself believe I would be following God in refusing; but when night came, things were different. "You must do it," God had told me. "Go to Pyongyang." Wasn't that kind, loving voice the power of God comforting and encouraging me, even though I was so frightened and weak? When I recalled His voice, my stubbornness began to melt away just like ice when hot water is poured upon it.

If the purpose of His voice was to tell me that I was to go with Elder Park to warn the Japanese government, could I live against His holy will? My agony deepened. Finally, the cold which I had had for some time developed into pneumonia, and I was confined to my bed. The pain in my chest was severe, and my breathing was difficult. I seemed to be wandering miserably at the bottom of my agony.

Deep coughs shook my entire body, and my sputum was scarlet with blood. A shadow of sadness was on my mother's face as the doctor came and examined me. Not long before, I had prayed for death. Now I feared it.

"There is not much difference between pneumonia and being beaten and kicked," Mother said to me. "Concerning your going to warn the Japanese authorities, I can think of many things that make me feel that God has planned this for you since you were a child."

I knew she was speaking the truth, but my weakness and lack of faith were causing me to deceive myself into going the wrong way. Finally I yielded my will to His.

"Mother," I said, "I am ready to listen to the Lord. Even though I may have to die on the way, I will go to Japan and warn her people with God's Word."

Feebly I got out of bed, took my best silk clothes from the chest, put on some makeup, combed my hair, and went out to the main street. It was a bitter winter morning, and the air was like ice. I was coughing so hard and shaking so hard that I thought I would surely lose my balance and fall to the pavement. But I boarded a taxi and got off in front of the city's most luxurious department store, where crowds were always passing. Choosing a place where I could easily be seen, I closed my eyes to pray.

"Lord, if You have truly chosen me to warn the Japanese government, prove it clearly to me. If the people suddenly stop and look at me in surprise, I will believe that You have given my face a special glow. Then I will follow Your voice unto death and go to Japan."

Opening my eyes wide, I watched the crowd walking by, waiting for somebody to notice me and to indicate by their look of surprise that there was a special glow on my face. But no one acted as though they saw me. I was trembling and coughing so much in the freezing cold that I could not lift my head and was about to collapse. When I got home, disappointed and shaking miserably, I burst into tears. My mother seemed to understand.

"You read your Bible," she told me, "but you want to do what the Bible does not say. Jonah did not pray for a sign when he went to the city of Nineveh to warn the people to repent of their sins. Esther did not ask for a sign before she approached the king. It is wrong and dangerous to ask God for what the Bible does not say. The Bible is our guide."

I made up my mind to fast once more. In my weakened condition, the three-day fast was extremely difficult and I felt as though I was almost dying. However, when I had completed the fast, I knew I had not been able to do it in my own strength.

Before dawn on the third day, I looked at the Bible in the dim light. The print on the page suddenly grew in size and became so bright that it seemed to leap into my eyes as though each word were fitted with wings. I was enchanted as these verses from Ezekiel sprang to meet my startled gaze:

> "Son of man, stand on your feet. . . . I am sending you to . . . a rebellious people who have rebelled against Me; they . . . are stubborn and obstinate children; and you shall say to them, 'Thus says the Lord GOD.' As for them, whether they listen or not—for they are a rebellious house—they will know that a prophet has been among them. And you, son of man, neither fear them nor fear their words, though thistles and thorns are with you and you sit on scorpions; neither fear their words nor be dismayed at their presence, for they are a rebellious house. . . .

Son of man, listen to what I am speaking to you. . . ." Then I looked, behold, a hand was extended to me; and lo, a scroll was in it. . . . It was written on the front and back; and written on it were lamentations, mourning and woe (Ezekiel 2:1–10 NASB).

As the words came running out of the Bible and came close to my face, I could read them slowly. As I did so, I received strength, and a wave of joy filled my excited heart.

"I will tell them, even though they might hear or refuse!" I shouted, rejoicing. "I will not rebel like a rebellious house, O Lord."

My voice was so loud that my mother rushed to my bed. She brought me something to drink when I requested it to break my fast. When I told her what had happened, she was as content as ever. We read Ezekiel 2.

When we read the last verse, we knew that Japan would continue to rebel against God. However, now my mind was set. I would go to Tokyo with Elder Park and warn the high officials of the central government. I might be beaten or killed or imprisoned or starved, but it would be better than rebelling against God.

I knew my fate. I was sure that I would die at the hands of the Japanese.

10

SEEING, THEY DO NOT PERCEIVE

It was easy to see why Mother felt God had been preparing me to go to Tokyo to deliver His warning. My father had insisted that I be educated in Japan and had sent me there to college when I was eighteen. I had become as fluent in their language as I was in my native Korean, and I had great respect for my Japanese friends and teachers. I had learned to love the Japanese and was loved by them in return. Actually, during my years in Japan, I had thought of myself as being Japanese. The only thing that bothered me was their idol worship, and I tried to discover a way to teach them to know the true God. After I had graduated and gone back home to Korea, I had returned to Japan whenever I had a chance.

Within my heart, however, I knew this nation would surely perish and that the people would be destroyed by fire from heaven unless they turned away from idolatry and worshiped the living God with all their hearts. God had a purpose in having me love Japan. I knew He would help me to tell them what I had longed to say.

Elder Park was opposed to my fasting. "Doesn't God say

we should eat a lot and get busy?" he asked. "Why are you always sick?"

When I asked him about getting a passport the next day, he said that we wouldn't need one. We were ambassadors of God, sent to give a great warning to Japan, he declared, so we would not need a tiny piece of paper from the Japanese.

"Without a passport," I told him. "I can't go with you. The Bible tells us to keep the laws of the land."

For the first time I saw him flustered. "I can't go to the police department," he said. "If I go, I'll be jailed."

I could understand why he felt as he did. Besides, he was right; they would never give him a passport. Still, I could not go with him unless he did. He meditated for a long while before speaking. "Let me leave first," he said. "When I reach Seoul, I'll go to the deputy general."

We decided to meet at the Seoul station after three days. He did have a problem, however, for his clothing was too shabby for the trip. When I volunteered to buy him a new suit, he asked me to get him a tuxedo. He left for the capital city, carrying the new suit in a box under his arm. As for me, I would have an opportunity to wear the clothes my mother and sister had already prepared for my wedding. I picked out the most expensive clothing and put it into my suitcase; then I filled my large leather purse with money and was ready to go.

In spite of my recent problems with the police, I had no difficulty in obtaining a new passport. I had made many trips to Japan. Another presented no difficulties.

This, I felt, was my last farewell. I rejoiced as I thought that Jesus was not very far from me. When I returned home, several fellow believers were waiting for me. When night came, others drifted over until the house was filled with people. At Reverend Chae's suggestion, I read Ezekiel 2 and a verse from the book of Esther.

"I will go in to the king, which is not according to the law; and if I perish, I perish" (Esther 4:16 NASB). I repeated the final phrase once again. "If I perish, I perish."

Those who were gathered at our home repeated it after me, their faces shining with firm resolution. They, too, were looking forward to death. Some were unable to pray aloud because of tears, but their hearts were as one with my heart and they all prayed in their hearts for me.

Above everyone else, my mother was content and beautiful and filled with the Holy Spirit. What a wonderful woman she was!

The railway station was crowded since a special express train was leaving for the south. Most of the passengers were Japanese, accompanied by their families. Usually I bought a round-trip ticket so I would not have to worry about getting another to return. This time I did not bother; I was certain my life would end in Tokyo.

Believers had come to the station by various routes and at different times to avoid attracting attention, and when I went out on the platform I could see them raising their hands to give me the sign of faith. I raised my hand in return. Then I bowed my head to my Christian brothers and sisters as the train arrived.

"Lord, let me die like Your servant," I prayed.

When the train stopped at Seoul, Elder Park got on. He could not get a passport, he explained. I gave him the second-class ticket I had bought for him.

"We don't need those," he said, ignoring the ticket to Tokyo. It was obvious that he was having difficulty in restraining his laughter. "I mean, I don't need such a thing made by men since God is my refuge." I wished I were half as confident as he so that I could do my job without difficulty.

"Will you please try to understand what I'm saying to you?" I persisted. "I'm worried because you don't have a passport." I asked him to sit in another place in the coach so I would not be involved if he were arrested.

"You're expecting the worst," he said, grinning. "You're thinking of when we're found. You want me to go to the corner? I'll go. I'll go."

The special express train was nearing Pusan when four harbor policemen entered the coach. Two checked the tickets from my end while the other two started from the other end, not far from where Elder Park was sitting. Passports would be checked here for passengers going to Japan. I was passed without difficulty, but I was not concerned about myself. I looked back timidly, to see what was happening with Elder Park. I could scarcely believe it! The two policemen had already passed him. He was smiling broadly, his chin held high.

I couldn't understand it. Couldn't those policemen see that he didn't have a passport? They couldn't have made a mistake. Tokyo tickets were a different color, and he was the only passenger in the car who was dressed in the traditional Korean manner. Not only that, he was dressed so shabbily that his clothes shouted his presence.

Seeing that I was looking at him, he stood to come toward me, leaning on his cane. When he got close, he pushed two of the policemen aside and walked past the other two. One of the officers made a path for him without turning to look.

"They couldn't see me," he explained, laughing. "They all became blind. The Lord is my refuge!"

I felt nervous to hear him talk so loudly, fearing the police would hear him. When I put my finger to my lips to warn him to be silent, he stared reproachfully at me, twisting his fingers in his beard. "How unbelieving you are!" he said. "Don't you want to believe?"

He turned as though he were disturbed with me and went back to his own seat, again pushing the policeman out of his way. This time I was sure he would be discovered. But he moved as easily along the aisle as though there had been no officer in the coach and reached his own seat safely.

When we arrived at Pusan, I asked Elder Park to stay with my suitcase in an obscure corner while I exchanged my Korean money for Japanese yen. It took longer than I had expected, and when I hurried back to the place where I had left my friend, he was not there. For an instant fear seized me. I was sure the harbor policemen must have discovered him and had taken him away.

Unable to find a porter to help me, I dragged my suitcase across the pier. Only then did I see Elder Park. He was changing into his tuxedo, and a policeman was helping him!

I went even closer. When he saw me, he called out loudly in Korean, "Look, this policeman is kindly helping me. You see, I must clothe myself like God's ambassador."

The policeman did not seem to have understood what the old man said. He was still smiling as Elder Park kicked his tattered Korean clothes off the pier and into the sea. "I don't need such clothes any longer," he said.

The ferry whistle signaled that the time to board had arrived. Elder Park walked ahead of me to the gangplank. "You'll want to see this," he told me, going confidently aboard. Policemen were at the far end of the gangway, one on each side, but they let Elder Park pass without a question. I couldn't believe it, but he was aboard. That, I knew.

I was so stunned that I could not find my own ticket and passport when I was asked to show them. Nervously I went through my handbag and then my suitcase, but I could not locate them. Elder Park called out to me in Korean, "What's taking you so long? The boat is leaving!"

I must admit that I was furious at him. Why did he have to be so slow-witted? He was already aboard; he should have waited quietly. Then, of all things, he came down the gangway to join me.

"Why are you keeping her here so long?" he asked the policeman.

"She can't find her passport."

"Here," Elder Park said, "I'll look for it for you."

He snatched my purse from me, and in a moment or two he was able to find it.

When I finally got aboard, I looked for Elder Park but couldn't find him. One of the policemen noticed my nervousness and came over to me. "You must be looking for your father," he said.

I was so disturbed I couldn't answer him immediately.

When I could speak I tried to tell him not to bother, but he was already on his way. I was sure something terrible would happen this time, but in a few moments Elder Park and the officer approached me.

"When you roam around so much," the policeman told Elder Park, "your daughter feels nervous. You must stay closer to her." It wasn't long until he came back with some tea for me.

I recalled how the apostle Peter thought he was dreaming after an angel had released him from prison. I am sure I knew exactly how he felt. Elder Park looked very happy. "Jehovah is my refuge," he said.

The ship had already left port, and Pusan Harbor was shrinking in size as we plodded across the narrow stretch of sea. Not by chance had we been able to pass the Pusan harbor police; it was like escaping the gates of hell. Jehovah was alive and working within us. Joy and thanks filled my heart as I went out to the second-class veranda.

Dark clouds were moving fiercely across the vast sky, driven by strong winds and swollen with rain and snow. The ominous clouds stretched from horizon to horizon. Were they telling me that my way would be stormy and difficult? The sea was an earthy reflection of the raging sky. Around me I could see nothing calm, nothing peaceful, nothing beautiful.

The strong, stormy winds of the future were so threatening that it seemed almost impossible for me to see God's face. My heart, as dark as the clouds, felt as if it were sinking to icy depths. I lay down on the floor, miserable in my anxiety.

"Jesus!" I called the name of the Lord and wept loudly. My heart was burdened heavily, but I had no words to pray.

Raindrops as large as soybeans pelted down upon me, and the sound of the driving rain against the deck was like the sound of ten thousand carpenters noisily driving as many nails into the planking. The full force of the winter storm had hit the ferry, and we were lunging savagely into every breaker. I got to my feet and lurched toward the dry warmth of the cabin. My heart searched for the hands of God.

11

A MIRACLE
AND AN
OLD MAN

When we finally arrived at the Tokyo station, the platform was crowded as usual. When our train stopped, I saw a moon-faced youth with extremely large eyes standing near the window.

"My son!" Elder Park called out loudly. "There is my son, Yong Chang! Here is another miracle! In such a crowd as this, where is my son? Right in front of us! It is the same as it was when the Lord led me to you, Miss Ahn. How did my son know we were coming? Answer me!"

It was as Elder Park said: a miracle!

We asked the taxi driver to take us to a quiet, clean hotel. My large room on the fifth floor had a good view of the streets and stores. However, I was unable to sleep because of the cold. In the morning a maid brought in a brazier and a charcoal heater, but they provided only enough heat to warm my face and hands. I went down to the street and bought an electric heater, but that didn't help a great deal either. The effect of a hot bath lasted only as long as I was in the warm water. As soon as I got out of the tub, I was shivering and coughing. I was no longer coughing up blood, but the incessant coughing tired me. I did not see how someone as weak as I could carry on a great mission of God.

How often I had vowed confidently to God that I would give Him everything I possessed while I was still young, still beautiful, and full of strength. But now my faith had become weak. And now, how ugly and unseemly I had become. I was saddened by the thought that now I was offering to God this ugly, useless, wasted body. I was still deeply disturbed when Elder Park knocked on my door and entered.

"What's this for?" he asked, showing me a second-class ticket from Seoul to Tokyo.

I was upset at him. "You were supposed to give it to the station clerk when you went out of the Tokyo station," I said. "How did you ever get out without presenting it?"

"I showed it to him, but he was so busy collecting tickets from the others that he didn't see me. Someone pushed me from behind, and here I am with the ticket."

I shook my head. How could such a thing happen?

"Don't you see it yet?" he asked me. "The Lord is my refuge. God has blinded all the Japanese people in order to hide me from them. What can blind people see?"

I was thinking of the cold and the way it afflicted me. If God loved Elder Park so much as to blind the Japanese people, would He not work a miracle for me, too, in order to take away the penetrating coldness?

I opened the front window and looked down on the Tokyo business district of tall buildings standing, row upon row. And the people. Everywhere I looked there were people—pushing, shoving crowds of people. Not many of them knew about the colonization policy that was in effect in Korea. I was sure that not many government authorities and politicians knew and understood the cruel, merciless tyranny of the deputy general of Korea. Would people like that listen to what I was going to say? I asked the Lord how a frail woman such as I and an old man like Elder Park, who could hardly see and didn't know the Japanese language, would be able to do anything against so great a nation. We were like two gulls crying loudly into the teeth of the raging wind, trying to still its blowing.

"O Lord," I prayed, "look down on these two miserable sea gulls." Then these words from Psalm 73 helped me:

> But as for me, my feet came close to stumbling; my steps had almost slipped. For I was envious of the arrogant, as I saw the prosperity of the wicked. For there are no pains in their death; and their body is fat. They are not in trouble as other men; nor are they plagued like mankind. Therefore pride is their necklace; the garment of violence covers them. Their eye bulges from fatness; the imaginations of their heart run riot. . . . They have set their mouth against the heavens, and their tongue parades through the earth . . . They say, "How does God know?" . . . How they are destroyed in a moment! They are utterly swept away by sudden terrors! (vv. 2–7, 9, 11, 19 NASB).

Then a power lifted my heart and I could look up with courage. The sky was still dark and cloudy, and rain or snow threatened to fall at any moment. Once more I looked down at that seething mass of humanity. They were well fed, well clothed, and filled with confidence, but as I saw them a great sadness arose within my heart.

"Jesus!" I said to my Savior. "The crowd You saw must have been like this one. That was why You could not come down from the cross but had to die there. You died to save them. I shall also die. Even though I might have to go through horrible torture, I shall die gladly if that will make this crowd walk in the right path."

The sudden pouring rain interrupted my prayer. I closed the window and began to tremble again. Before spring came I would tell these Japanese all about the love of God. I would die for it and go to heaven where there would never be such cold wind or snow or cloudy days. It would always be warm and comfortable, and cool, breezy days would continue forever. Again I found strength to face the hours and days that lay ahead.

The following day we visited Lieutenant General Gunpei Yamamuro of the Salvation Army. He had been ill, but when we got to his office he was there and kindly consented to see us.

He was an aged man and so feeble that secretaries had to walk on either side, supporting him. They helped him to a large armchair in the center of the room and seated him. Then one of the secretaries introduced him. His face was expressionless, more like a wizened ceramic doll. I stood and introduced Elder Park and myself. I didn't want to reveal the true purpose of our visit to one so frail and in such poor health, but we were there and could not leave without saying something.

I asked him what he thought about a Christian who went to a pagan shrine and bowed there.

"I've never paid any attention to it," he said with a promptness that surprised me. I guess I expected him to be senile.

"Then, sir," I continued, "are you saying that it isn't a sin if a Christian worships the gods of Japanese Shintoism?"

"That is exactly what I am saying." He continued in a low, monotone voice. "I was raised in a small country town. When I grew up, I was sent to the battlefield with a friend of mine. He was killed and his body was buried at a local shrine. Whenever I go back to my hometown I visit the shrine, bow to my friend's tomb, and give thanks for his having died for our country. I am a Christian, but I don't consider that what I do is a sin."

I was stunned at his words. *What is the difference between a Christian and a non-Christian,* I thought, *if a believer does the same things as a nonbeliever? Why would he even become a Christian unless he allowed God to change his life?*

"How do you see present-day Japan?" I asked him. "Is your nation going in the right direction?"

It was difficult to answer that question, he told me, but he thought Japan was moving in a rather dangerous direction.

Summoning all the courage I possessed, I continued. "The newspapers and the radio say that Japan is going to conquer all of Asia. Let's face the facts. All the youth in Japan are being taken to the battlefields where they will die and go to hell. They do not know the way of salvation because nobody has told them about it. And the Japanese government is so blinded about the war that it cannot see what is happening."

I went on to tell him about the persecution that was coming to faithful pastors and men and women of God, but that no one had told the governing authorities about the problem. For that reason, God had called a sickly, weak individual like myself and the elderly man who was my companion, who did not know a single word of Japanese, to come and in obedience to warn the leaders, thus showing me how to obey God and die for His love.

"We are ready to die," I said, "but Japan will also suffer. She will soon be burned up by sulphur fire."

I thought he would be angry, but only sadness reflected in his sunken eyes. "I used to have the duty of blessing the emperor once a month," he said. "To do it, I went to the palace, but now I am unable to do anything. But I ask you to pray for me."

My heart ached as I opened my Bible and read some verses from the book of Jeremiah to show him how Japanese Shintoism resembled Baal worship. He listened with astonishment.

"Please pray for me," he said. "And I will pray that God will use you to waken Japan and lead her to repentance."

My storming emotions turned to tears of sadness. The Salvation Army lieutenant general had been given such a high position that he was able to visit the emperor regularly. How God must have wanted him to testify of the truth to Japan. Now his health was destroyed, and he realized that Japan was threatened with destruction but he could do nothing about it. Many respectable leaders were in the nation, but they had no idea of the wrongs being carried out.

"I must speak!" I said again. I would convey God's loving warning to this people, even though it might require my life.

As a nation, Japan was an enemy of our beloved Korea. But as human beings created by God, these people were our brothers and sisters. God wanted to use me to save them. Life in this world would be brief for me, but hell is eternal.

12

A SYMPATHETIC EAR

Among all of the Japanese authorities, the most familiar name to us was that of the former deputy general of Korea, General Kazunari Ugaki. Since he knew and respected our people and had ruled with a tolerant hand, we felt it would be well for us to meet and talk with this admirable statesman. We found his number in the phone book, learned that he was at his villa in a suburb west of Tokyo, and went out to see him. It was midafternoon when I presented my card to his secretary.

He stared at it in surprise or fear and bowed so politely that I was uncomfortable. In Japan, as is true in the rest of the world, it is impossible to meet famous, influential people without going through complicated procedures. But God was with us. The general's personal secretary must have supposed that I was a member of the Ei royal family, for he accorded us the honor due a person in that exalted position. He invited us to wait until General Ugaki returned from his walk in an hour.

We could have waited inside, but I told Elder Park I wanted to be alone so I could pray. My heart was heavy and I wanted to tell my Lord about it. I went out onto the Musashino Plain, a vast, flat area covered with overgrown reeds that rustled in the strong wind. Walking along a narrow, twisting path, I felt as though I were in a forest. I could see nothing except the path ahead.

I don't know why, but I climbed a big pine tree that thrust its shaggy head high above the undulating sea of reeds. I wanted only to find a quiet place where I could pray. Coming abreast of the tree, I turned impulsively and began to climb, using the branches as though they were rungs on a ladder.

I hadn't realized the protection the reeds afforded until I climbed above them and was buffeted by the savage wind. My fingers tightened convulsively on one limb after another until I reached a heavy crotch that gave me some protection against the icy gale.

The pine tree was crying mournfully, echoing my heart's desolation. I knew I could not be heard above the soughing wind, so I cried out my agony in my shrill soprano voice, sharing with Jesus all the hurt and frustration and fear that encompassed my heart.

I had never been afraid to die. Even now that we were about to embark on the course I was sure would lead to my death, I was not afraid. But I was terrified of the torture and cruelty that would surely be my lot as soon as I was imprisoned. Never before had I experienced such desperation.

I didn't even notice a young man approaching until he called to me from the tree's base, signaling with his hand for me to come down. I tried to descend, but I could not. I had clung so tightly and for so long to the branch that I could not release my fingers. The young man, who must have been concerned about me, again motioned for me to come down. By this time I was so cold and so much time had passed that I, too, wanted to get on the ground again. I had never been so exasperated or felt so helpless. But try as I would, I could not so much as move one finger. Still clinging to the tree limb, I slid free of the crotch until I was hanging by my hands. Gradually the weight of my body overcame my locked fingers and I slipped free, falling to the ground. I couldn't help wondering what the general would have thought had he come upon me when I was in the tree or hanging from the branch.

When the time came for Elder Park and me to see General Ugaki, we were led to a room to wait for him. A moment later he entered quietly, a gentle, kindly man who looked more like a friend of my father's than I expected a great leader to appear.

He confirmed my suspicion that his secretary had thought I was from the royal Ei family. His voice made me remember his visit to a school in Korea where I was teaching. "You're the youngest teacher," he had said to me. "Don't work too hard." I had liked him then, and now I felt as though he were truly a friend. I informed him that I was not related to the royal family, nor was I a noble.

"I was educated in Japan and am only one of the Christians making an effort to live in faith." He listened carefully as I continued. "I have received a special task from God. This elderly man here with me has the same task, but I must do the speaking, since he does not know the Japanese language. Yet, God called him to help me so I would not fear nor fail to accomplish the task." The words stopped in my throat. I had difficulty in telling him the purpose of our visit. "God has sent me to warn Japan."

I saw the warmth and understanding in his features. He was even more friendly than before when he assured me that I need not be afraid. "There is nothing wrong for you to tell me whatever you want," he said. "So tell me anything you have in mind." He was old and spoke slowly. "At present I have no power. I don't even have a name that will command a hearing with the people, but the authorities of the present government are my friends. They will listen to me. I think I will be able to help you."

That encouraged us, and I contrasted the difference between Korea during his regime and the situation under the new governor general.

"When you were ruling, everyone could worship God freely as Christians," I told him. "But now believers are hated and persecuted more than murderers. Those who have been able to escape from the police wander in the mountains and caves, while their families are scattered like beggars, roaming from town to town." I went on to tell him that true believers could never worship the shrine, for that is a violation of God's commandments. I told him the devout whose faith was strong were being brutally persecuted, while the weak were enticed to become spies and play the part of Judas, betraying their more courageous brothers. "God has clearly told me," I concluded, "that Japan will be punished and be burned and destroyed by sulphur rain unless she repents and turns from this course of destruction."

When I finished, the general nodded as if in agreement. "I was one of the candidates for prime minister," he said. "And if I had been elected I would have done my very best for our nation. But the military is so strong that my friends who were supporting me were reluctant to continue to back me. For that reason I have no direct authority. However, that does not mean that I am without friends and influence. I will have to be careful in what I say, but most of my friends in the government are grieving for Japan's future. At this moment the situation is most dangerous."

Sensing his agony for Japan, I was bold enough to dare to ask him what he thought of the Bible.

"I studied in Germany," he answered without hesitation. "My landlady was a devout believer who read the Bible at the breakfast table and always prayed before every meal. I had deep respect for her, and consequently a deep interest in the Bible."

I presented him with an inexpensive Bible I had bought that morning. He thanked me and opened it thoughtfully.

"I shall read it every day," he promised.

As we left, bending against the strong north wind that tore at my hair, a splendid orchestra was performing magnificently and solemnly in my heart.

I shall die, I thought. *I shall die to obey His will!*

13

A BROKEN
APPOINTMENT

Sunday we went to the service at Fujimi-cho Church. After the simple and comparatively short service, I went up to the pastor and asked him if Major General Hibiki was attending the service that morning. While I was still talking to the minister, an elegant old man with gray hair and a moon-shaped baby face was passing by. Pastor Miyoshi stopped him and introduced me to the man I wanted to see. I asked if I could talk to him.

He took me to a quiet little room and asked me to be seated. "Now," he said, "what is it you wish to see me about?"

"I'm excited and happy at being able to worship God in a church after such a long time," I said. "There is no longer such a thing as the Lord's Day in Korea."

His face twisted quizzically. "What do you mean, there is no Lord's Day in Korea?"

"The churches can no longer worship God. It's the same as having no Lord's Day." I didn't want to cry, but I could not help it. "Hundreds of churches have become factories for military uniforms, taken over by force," I said. "A miniature shrine is placed in the center of the altar, and policemen are always present to see that believers do not come to worship God without bowing to the shrine."

I went on to say that pastors were forced to speak on political and social subjects rather than about the Gospel. "Offerings and bells have been confiscated, and Christians who have refused to worship the shrine have been forced to flee to escape being imprisoned and tortured and killed."

The stately officer blinked his round eyes and was so agitated that his voice thundered. "What in the world are you talking about?"

"Since Governor Minami took over, he has launched a five-year program of Japanization. He has forced people to change their Korean names for Japanese names and forbidden the use of the Korean language."

His face reddened in anger. "Foolish Minami! Is he such an idiot?"

I had never imagined that Major General Hibiki, who was loved and respected by all the high-ranking officials, and the only surviving officer from the Russo-Japanese War, would abuse Governor Minami so quickly. Being a military man, he seemed to be impatient, though he was old.

"I believe God is speaking to me through you, but I can't listen to you alone. Come, let's go to Matsuyama's."

He went to the office, made a phone call, and we left the church to go to the residence of Congressman Tsunejiro Matsuyama by car.

"Now," Major General Hibiki said to me, "tell him what you have already told me. Tell us everything that you have seen or heard."

I was scarcely conscious that two very important Japanese men were listening to me. God was giving me the words to say. While I was talking, both of them seemed to be struck silent by the information I was relating to them. It was obvious that they did not know what was going on in Korea.

"I would like to have the top political leaders hear you,"

Congressman Matsuyama said when I finished. Like General Ugaki and General Hibiki, he was deeply disturbed by the danger of the military gaining more power. "We must have as many representatives as possible to hear this before the religious bill is passed."

"Yes," General Hibiki agreed, "that is absolutely necessary."

The two men set to work immediately, telephoning the representatives, most of whom were at home preparing for the Seventy-fourth Imperial Diet.* Finally, the schedule was arranged. General Hibiki handed it to Elder Park's son, who was attending a seminary in Tokyo, and gave him instructions for the meeting.

The representatives were too busy the next day to even take time for breakfast. The schedule called for the first appointment to be at five in the morning. That meant we would have to be up by three A.M.

"It has been very difficult to make the appointments," he warned us. "Don't be late by even a minute."

I looked over the schedule when we were alone. Each appointment was for five minutes. It was probably only because of the reputations of the men requesting the time that we were able to get in to see them at all. God had shown us again that He was directing our venture in Japan.

Elder Park's son went to the International Hotel for the night, while we went back to our own hotel. I was so concerned that I couldn't go to sleep. While waiting for dawn, I spent the time praying.

Elder Park was up at 3:30. He paced back and forth in front of my room and coughed politely in order to waken me. I got up and opened the window. The sky was still dark, and the stars were twinkling weakly in the cloudy sky.

Elder Park's son was supposed to come at 3:30. It was almost 4 o'clock when his father and I went out into the corridor. When 4:30 came, we were desperate. Elder Park's anger

*The Diet met from Dec. 1938 to Mar. 1939.

81

flared and he spoke darkly of striking his son when he did appear. I cried to the Lord, but still the young man did not come. Even at 5 o'clock, there was no sign of him.

I felt like jumping out of the window to kill myself because I was so ashamed. Those two busy men had tried so earnestly to save their country and had given us the opportunity to speak to the very persons who had the power to change the entire course of events. We had failed them. We were utterly irresponsible.

"O Lord," I cried out in agony. "If I am truly Your child, take me to the other world right now. O God, my God, that is the only way."

A severe pain developed in my chest, and I longed for death. During the night, I had been unable to sleep. Now, without knowing it, I fell asleep. I was awakened by the angry voice of Elder Park as he scolded his son for oversleeping and causing us to miss those very important appointments. I noted the time. It was nine o'clock. Just then the phone rang.

"What is this?" General Hibiki demanded angrily. "Who are you trying to make a fool of?"

Actually, I welcomed his scolding. I even wished that he would abuse me with harsher words. I was weeping as he talked.

"Are you listening?" he demanded. "Are you listening to me?"

"Yes. Yes, sir!"

"Why do you keep silent?"

"I can't speak. Your excellency, I shall write to you right now by special delivery."

"By special delivery?" he repeated. That did nothing to ease his anger.

I wrote a letter with quick brush strokes, explaining all that had happened. After two and a half hours the phone rang. I picked up the receiver but heard no voice. I began to weep again. Moments later, I heard a crying voice saying over and over again, "Pardon me. Pardon me." It was General Hibiki.

Finally he blurted, "Would you please come and see me to-day?"

It was a strange conversation. He was crying so hard that his sobs vibrated in the receiver. I was crying until I could not answer him.

"Would you please see me today?" he asked. "Please. There are many things I want to talk to you about."

We decided to meet in a popular Tokyo park near the east entrance. When I got there, that 81-year-old military man was waiting for me, his thin frame erect. Somehow, he looked like one of the aged pastors in the underground church who was longing for the love of the Lord and aiming for martyrdom. He took my hand as I bowed politely, and had me sit where he had been sitting to wait for me.

We were both silent for a time, but our hearts were in perfect understanding. His anger and my sorrow both came from the same source. We wanted to save this people and nation. We had been given new lives by the same righteous God and were bound together by the same purpose and grief. Yet, a misunderstanding stood like a wall between us.

"I have lived for eighty-one years," he began, "but never have I had a day when I was so moved as I have been today." He took out a large white handkerchief and wiped his eyes. "I dislike tears in a man. It's too womanish. But today I have been crying all day long. It probably is the work of the Holy Spirit."

I also was crying at the time.

"I have a favor to ask you."

"Yes, General."

"You are loved and used by God," he went on. "Would you please become my adopted daughter? You could study at the seminary and work more for God."

I did not know what to say to him. To become a daughter of this beloved Major General! How wonderful that would be! And to become a seminary student and study about the God I loved! It would have given me everything I had ever wanted or dreamed about from life. But at the same time I recalled the words that Satan had whispered to Jesus. "All these things will I give You, if You fall down and worship me" (Matthew 4:9 NASB).

"I am living alone," he said, "being taken care of by a man servant. I've been praying and seeking a way in which I could serve God by spreading the Gospel to all my people. I think you are the person to help me to carry out that task.

"It isn't necessary that you die to serve the Lord. It is more important to live righteously and to tell people that Jesus Christ is the only way of salvation. I know you're thinking it is difficult to evangelize the Japanese; but with your faith and ability to impress others, you will be able to do much for God. And, since you are young, it isn't too late to enter the seminary for study."

He stopped, and I became aware that he had finished and I would have to speak. "You think I am a living person," I told him, "but I am already dead. The moment I stood up for this task, I, Ahn Ei Sook, was dead and became a corpse. What can such a corpse do?"

There was a lengthy silence. He wiped his eyes incessantly with his large white handkerchief. "God has saved me and has been very good to me," he said, "but there is nothing I have done for God. I am ashamed of myself. What have I done up to this day? Now, at the close of my long life, I only feel sorry to God as a believer—"

As we cried together, I felt that Jesus was standing there with us.

The evening had advanced, and the cloudy sky was growing darker with each passing minute. Knowing that he must have been very tired, I stood and walked slowly with him to his car.

14

A CHALLENGE
TO THE OPPRESSORS

It was March 23, 1939, and the final session of the Seventy-fourth Imperial Diet was nearing adjournment. The bill of religious organization had been presented to the legislators and was still to be voted on. Elder Park insisted that we disregard the laws of the nation and fight illegally.

"We have to go to the Diet, drop down our bill of warning from the balcony, and shout out the truth so everyone will hear," he said fervently.

"We'll be arrested!"

"Without doubt we will be arrested," he replied. "And there will be a hearing. That is the only way we can appeal to the law and reveal the sort of decision the court would hand down in Korea."

I was strongly against it. By deliberately acting like criminals, we would be misunderstood. And, as lowly prisoners, we would never be able to give our warning.

"Who would listen to convicted criminals?" I asked him. "Who would recognize us as apostles of Jesus?"

Still, I was undecided. We could not conclude that Elder

Park's way was not God's will just because it did not agree with my nature. Hundreds of believers in Korea were praying that God would guide us and give us wisdom. The only safe way was to leave the matter to the wisdom of our Lord.

The next morning Elder Park didn't come down for breakfast, and that was unusual for him. I went to his room and found him hard at work, brushing large Chinese characters on a sign that was to be a warning to the Diet.

1. The Japanese government should repent and withdraw its tyranny from Korea.
2. Examine which is the true religion—Shintoism or Christianity.
3. Burn a stack of wood and throw a Shinto believer and myself into it. The one who is not burned shall prove the true religion.

When Elder Park insisted that this was the only action left to us as Koreans, his expression said that he was determined to die. I was afraid for him and for myself. But if the time had come for me to die, what would it matter if I was imprisoned or broke the Japanese law? I would die as I had wished to do for so very long. I would stand erect and face my persecutors. I would die beautifully for the Lord, forsaking myself, my personality, my ideals. I would not look to death as an escape, because I hated this world.

Jesus had been leading us to the way of righteousness. He was our righteousness. I would leave everything in His hands.

That morning we went to the Diet building where we were informed that we had to have a letter of introduction from a representative. Congressman Matsuyama's secretary provided us with the necessary credentials.

When I entered the building through the entrance reserved for women, a female guard took everything I was carrying to check it until I returned. Rapidly she ran her hands over my clothing and examined my hair and my ears and even had me open my mouth so she could be sure I was not concealing anything on my person. I was not even allowed to take a pencil or a handkerchief into the gallery. Again, as though she were afraid she may have missed something, she frisked my body until it began to tickle and I started to giggle.

Elder Park and his son had already entered through the opposite door, and I met them on the third floor. With my eyes I signaled to him, and we sat together in the front row. There were uniformed guards everywhere.

When all of the seats were filled under the watchful eyes of the security officers, one of the guards informed us politely that we would have to remain seated once the Diet started. We were not supposed to look around or whisper to our neighbors. We were told not to laugh or cough or even raise our hands or turn our necks.

A speech by Representative Ando impressed me greatly.

"The spirit of religion is mercy and love," he said, "but it also is something that arms cannot conquer and wealth and nobility cannot ruin. It is powerful and fearless, daring to go against thousands. However, among the religious people today there are many who depend unreasonably upon the authorities. Compared with the fervent spirit of martyrdom of the founders of every great religion, such as Buddha and Christ, I cannot but wonder if the religious followers of today feel ashamed of themselves. I want to take this opportunity to urge religious people to reconsider themselves."

Listening to this legislator, I thought of Christ's reference to the salt that lost its flavor. That was true of so many believers everywhere.

While this was going on, Elder Park, who was sitting next to me, was trying to get something from his trouser leg. He had managed to get his bill of warning into the gallery and was trying to remove it from its hiding place so he could carry out his plan.

But today was not the day!

Representative Matsuyama had furnished us with the

letters of introduction that got us into the Diet chambers. We would be causing him great trouble if we were caught, which was sure to happen. Watching the guard carefully, I managed to whisper to Elder Park. "Not today. Let's go out quickly!"

I didn't give him an opportunity to argue with me. I stood immediately and left the balcony, with him and his son following me. My gray-haired companion was upset and scolded me because I had stopped him just as he was ready to lay out the bill of warning.

"We do not need a powerless religion," Representative Ando had said. And how true that was. The Gospel of Christ was all-powerful. And the reason many believers did not have power was that their faith was dead. "It is the power of God unto salvation to every one that believeth" (Romans 1:16), Paul had written. The words Elder Park had painted with his brush were also a testimony of the power of his faith. It was the power of faith that caused a weakling like myself to dare to follow Jesus without fearing death.

Representative Ando had been referring to that kind of faith. He had been urging the Japanese people to accept it, but they would not. Instead of seeking it, they kicked it away.

The next morning we got up rather early and went to breakfast together. I had not been able to sleep, for I was still anxious in my heart about breaking the law.

"Do you really think this is the way God has chosen?" I asked.

Elder Park was angry and impatient with me. "What?" he echoed. "Why don't you refuse if you don't want to die?" With that, he and his son left the table.

I had to go with them. Who could say that this was not the way God had prepared for us? I asked them to wait until I got into warmer clothes and picked up my Bible.

We had to go through the same procedure which we had followed the previous day. This time, however, we got our letters of introduction from the secretary of the Korean representative. We had decided we would rather cause trouble for him than for our Japanese friend. Elder Park and his son sat on the front row. I was in the row behind them.

The moment the declaration was finished, Elder Park took out the bill of warning and threw it down to the assembly hall. "Jehovah's great commission!" he shouted.

The bill of warning floated slowly to the floor of the assembly hall. The representatives watched it and waited to catch it with their upraised hands. A great roar went up, and Elder Park was seized by the guards and taken away. His son followed them. I closed my eyes and prayed.

"Lord," I told Him, "this was done. May it be Your will!"

Like Peter following Christ the night in which He was seized by the high priest, I went along, too, at a distance. When the guards asked if I was with Elder Park and his son, I told them I was. I, too, was arrested by the authorities.

"Lord," I prayed, my heart calm and peaceful, "I have accomplished the task You gave me."

The detective told us he was taking us to a third-class hotel. But it wasn't third class; it wasn't even a hotel. The sign above the entrance proclaimed Metropolitan Police Headquarters.

I was frightened.

15

BRIMSTONE FIRE WILL FALL!

I had never been in a prison before, but I was to learn there was an ugly sameness about all of them. The cells were not always alike, but they had the same purpose: restraint.

In this particular section of the jail, the cells were constructed of heavy iron-barred walls and barred doors which were arranged in a circle with a formidable iron fence encompassing them. The guardhouse near the entrance was high enough to give the men on patrol an unrestricted view of each prisoner at all times.

My coat, my handbag, and everything else I owned except for my skirt and blouse were taken away from me, and I was put in a solitary cell in a far corner. Elder Park and his son were jailed in the same way. There was a coldness in the prison beyond the chill of winter that weighed on my heart.

The icy cold of the concrete floor, the bars, and the frigid air was already cruel torture to me. My entire being shook from it. Although I tried to ignore it, it was impossible. Closing my eyes, I told God exactly how I felt.

For supper we got half a bowl of soup and a tiny bowl half

filled with a mixture of rice and wheat. It seemed to be just enough to keep the prisoners alive.

"Now I will walk in the valley of the shadow of death," I said to myself. "Take the hands of Jesus firmly. Look up to Him. Set your eyes on Him, believing His Word and trusting the guidance of the Holy Spirit. Since Ahn Ei Sook is dead, you must not live by your emotions in the way which the living do."

I sat up straight and coughed constantly in spite of the fact that the jailer watched me sharply. It seemed as though coughing was prohibited too.

The stern, unrelenting expression of the jailer with his vulgar speech and sharp eyes that missed nothing in that miserable place made my head ache. When night came, I curled up on one of the icy straw mats. My feet were like stumps, and I kept on coughing. I was still coughing when morning came.

I thought of myself as a child of sin with no power as a human being. God had used me for His service. Finally I had accomplished the task He had appointed for me. I was grateful, and tears of joy coursed down my quivering cheeks.

After a time I was taken to an interrogation room where a nervous, impetuous, merciless detective queried me so harshly that I was frightened. He threw the words at me contemptuously. "You lawless Koreans disturbed the Diet of holy, imperial Japan. You hindered the assembly of our great national leaders!"

"Mr. Detective," I said to myself. "What are you saying to a dead person?"

He asked me why I had come to Tokyo. Gratitude and joy rolled over me in great, comforting waves. I had missed the opportunity to speak to the government ministers and representatives because Elder Park's son had overslept. Now this new opportunity was being given to me. Was this the plan God had all along?

"Speak up!" the interrogator demanded angrily. "Why did you come to Tokyo?"

"Japan is at present rebelling against God, the Creator of the universe," I told him firmly. "God has to punish Japan. I have been sent here to tell the national leaders that Japan is going to be ruined by sulphur fire!"

"How could you think such a crazy thing?" he demanded, looking at me as if I were insane. "Do you believe what you say?"

"It is a pronouncement from God," I said.

"You fool!" he exploded. He wanted to know how we got into the building, who had given us letters of introduction, and whom we had seen before we went to the Diet building.

"I visited Major General Yanamuro," I related, "General Ugaki, Major General Hibiki, and Representative Matsuyama. They listened to me. Therefore, I came to the Diet to give the warning." I emphasized the fact that the Japanese leaders we had seen had only listened to me. I didn't want to cause trouble for them.

"Is this true?" the detective demanded.

"Why should I lie?"

"It was a crazy thing you did!" He turned to the detective who was taking notes. "She seems to be an important character," he whispered.

"Sulphur rain!" the other detective mocked. "She's crazy!"

16

UNDER
WATCHFUL EYES

I had been imprisoned for a month when I was taken to the visiting room where my sister was waiting to see me. I ran to her and threw my arms around her. The guard should not have permitted it, but he did.

My sister had brought her daughter to Tokyo to find a suitable college for her, and while she was there she read an article about Elder Park and me. She had remained in Tokyo to find out about us. It was so good to see her. I thanked God for the privilege of seeing someone in my family and hearing about Mother and the underground church.

My sister had given me food and new clothes, and then she handed me a large sum of money. "Use this as you need it," she said.

"Look," I said to her, seeing the dark veil of clouds break to let the sun shine through, "the sun is smiling at me. It is greeting me." I was as happy as a little child.

"Jesus is smiling," she said proudly.

My heart was filled with great happiness, and I worshiped Him with love and thankfulness.

When we were finally sent home to Korea from Japan, we were followed closely by three plainclothes policemen who carried my suitcases. I took the three second-class tickets my sister had bought for Elder Park, his son, and me, and we boarded the train. Looking out the window, I started singing and praising the Lord. The policemen wrote down everything we did or said, and they wouldn't let us walk together when we went to the buffet at noon for lunch.

"We're getting more and more famous," I said to the one who seemed to be assigned to me. I was just teasing him, but he wrote it down at once.

Our guards were changed at Nagoya. The new men hastily read the notes made by the detectives who had accompanied us from Tokyo and watched us carefully. I could not understand why they, too, made notes on our conversation, but every change of guards did the same. We constantly had three watching us on the trip from Tokyo to the ferry. At Shimonseki where we took the boat, our guards were increased to five. Once on land, our guard was again reduced to three.

At first we didn't know where we were being taken, but Elder Park and his son were taken to their native town, while I was taken to Bhak Chon, the place where I was born and grew up. A plainclothes detective and a uniformed policeman were with me. The officer in charge of the office of Bhak Chon County was angry and arrogant.

"You are the one who made a big disturbance that upset the police of imperial Japan and Korea! And you are the daughter of Ahn Choong Ho?" He sounded as though he could not believe a child of so respected a citizen as my father could be involved in such trouble.

"I know your father well," he said. "I don't want to say anything to you. You've had such a good education, you could have done something far better." He directed the detective to send me home.

Great joy arose in my heart when I arrived home and looked around the house. This household had gone through great turmoil when I was a child. Excessively sensitive and as strong willed as my father, I had my hair cut like a boy's because I hated having it combed. I didn't realize my rebellion at the time, but I was a thin, crop-headed girl who looked like a boy, brought trouble to the house, and pecked at the idols of my domineering grandmother. She was a zealous idol worshiper and had built a sizable altar so she could display and worship them in our home. Every season she would invite in the chief idol worshiper who lived in the area, as well as the soothsayers and astrologists, to a festival.

Even as a little girl I wondered why my grandmother, who was the most religious person I had ever seen, could be so filled with complaints and unhappiness. It seemed that she was always sick and discontented. Gradually I understood that her idols were the cause of her misery and lack of peace. On one occasion the preparations had been completed for the festival; the food was in the storage room, and a guard protected it. I slipped into the room when he wasn't looking and stood in front of the food that was to be offered to idols.

"You devils!" I exclaimed bitterly. "Why do you eat the best foods and then make my grandmother unhappy? Die eating the food mixed with my spittle!"

Saying this, I rubbed each of the foods with the spittle on my finger. If I had been discovered, which I wasn't, Grandmother and her daughters would have said I was the cause of her getting even sicker, that I had angered the idols. I was so irritated myself that I had to do something more. I had a servant bring Grandmother's walking stick to me. I put horse dung on the end and, touching each idol basket with it, said, "You demons! Why can't you make happiness and peace? Why do you make Grandmother unpleasant and upset while she worships you? Eat horse droppings and die!"

The servant was trembling with fright, but I was as pleased as Grandmother was shocked and angry. I thought the demons were dead, for sure. Although Grandmother was upset with me, certain members of my family were proud of me.

I started to receive a lot of attention at church and in town. My mother and sister, who were Christians, began to watch my behavior closely. On one occasion just before I went to sleep, my mother said to me, "As you can see, idols have no power at all. The Lord Jesus is the only One who can give us true power and happiness and peace."

Her words became a source of strength for me.

Idol worshipers whispered fearfully that on a rainy night the gods all walked out of their baskets to roam around the yard. For that reason everyone was frightened and no one wanted to go out in the yard if it was raining.

I was curious to see how the gods in the baskets looked, so I wrapped myself in a black blanket and waited behind the chimney to see them when they came out. About that time a servant came to the house from my father's office to get some food. He saw a black object moving behind the chimney and was sure he was seeing one of the gods. Screaming in terror, he fell to the ground and everyone dashed out to see what had happened. I was curious, too, and came out from behind the chimney. Then they all shouted their fright.

On another rainy night my cousin Kame was staying alone with a maid. I had asked her to go to Sunday school with me many times, but her mother was so bitterly opposed that she wouldn't let her. That night I wrapped myself in black and visited her. The gate was locked, so I climbed the fence and went into the yard.

"Kame!" I called. "Kame!"

She was scared, as I thought she would be.

"I am a god from the basket, Kame," I said.

I went into the house. Both my cousin and the maid turned as pale as linen. "Help!" the maid screamed. "Help! Have mercy on us, gods!"

Kame fainted.

"It's me, Kame," I told her. "It's Chung Sim (my nickname as a child). I'm not a god from the basket."

But it was no use. They were so sure they had been visited

by the gods, that they wouldn't listen to me. I went home crying. My uncle's family was very cautious about me after that night. I wished very much that Kame would also become a Christian, but she wouldn't listen to me.

On a cold winter night I had a dream so clear and vivid that I thought it was reality. I saw that Kame was coming up the hill where I stood. On the left side of the hill there was a smith shop where four men of dark-hued skin were blowing a fire and the red iron was giving off sparks. She had a lovely red ribbon in her black hair and looked as beautiful as ever. Knowing she was in danger, I warned her as loudly as I could.

Again I shouted to her that the men were evil and she might get burned by the fire. But she continued in the direction of the smith shop. I cried out to her with all my strength, but my voice could not reach her. She was getting closer and closer to the place of destruction.

I was warning her a third time when suddenly she fell toward the smith shop, and the four dark men drew her in.

"Oh, Kame! Kame!"

I cried so loudly that my own voice woke me from my dream. I was crying and trembling, and my mother came in to comfort me. She was still there when we heard a knock at the outer door.

"I'm from youngest uncle," a servant's voice called out. "I have come to tell you that his daughter, Kame, has died."

While skating on the river, she had caught a cold which developed into acute pneumonia. As for me, the entire earth darkened. My heart was tormented for a long time.

I had always loved Bhak Chon, a pretty little town with the crystal-clear water of the Tarung River running along it. The towering Won Su Bong Mountain rose sharply from the riverbank, and, as the water tumbled down the steep slope, it divided into a number of waterfalls.

Grandmother loved the mountain and often had her boat rowed there. She would load it with food and gather a number of her elderly friends in order to entertain them pompously. Several times I went with her.

The people in our town often said a hero would be born there because both the mountain and the river were magnificently beautiful.

Now, as I returned, all my friends with whom I had played and studied and had gone to church, were grown up. I had no way of knowing where they were or what they were doing. My father, influential as he was, was now getting old like a fading flower, and his clear, strong voice was becoming more gentle. I wondered how he would greet me, but he welcomed me warmly and was happy to see me.

The house looked entirely different, but I cherished it. My father showed me great kindness, but I sank into a terrible melancholy. I felt that I no longer had anything to do with this house. The world had changed. Oh, how everything had changed!

I left Bhak Chon after a week. The detective and policeman were almost too polite to me, which showed how influential my father had been in the town. When the train arrived at Pyongyang station, a uniformed officer and a detective were waiting for us. I was handed over to them, and they, too, were gracious and understanding. I was a prisoner, but I was being treated like a heroine with a police escort.

"Do you know how many officers had to write reports on you?" the chief supervisor asked me when I was ushered into his office in the high police division headquarters. "Do you have any idea how much the government has been forced to spend on you? Do you know how many long-distance calls had to be made? Are you aware of the fact that it required fifty-six policemen just to send you back here under guard?"

I could not offer an apology. I firmly believed that I had accomplished a task God had assigned to me. Therefore, I felt no regret. I stood in silence until he asked me to be seated.

At that moment a supervisor brought in an old man with a long white beard. His eyes were clear, and peace softened his lined features. Obviously he was not an ordinary prisoner.

"Go home and rest well," the vice supervisor told him.

The old man gathered up his few belongings and left. Again it was clear that he was different from the other prisoners. He didn't bow down many times like so many would have done, nor did he speak. Yet, he did not show any bitterness or arrogance.

"Do you know him?" the supervisor asked me. "Don't you know Pastor Ki Sun Lee?"

I had often heard of the pastor's bold faith and the spirit of martyrdom that governed his life, but I had never met him because he had been in jail when I had been in Pyongyang earlier. Now I had actually seen him being released!

I was given the same orders he had been given. "Go home and rest well, but when you move or go on a trip, you must report to us first."

A uniformed policeman and a detective followed me. When I got home Mother came running out to meet me in her bare feet. "Oh!" she exclaimed. "Oh!" She was so overjoyed she was unable to say more. Then she saw the officers and politely asked them, "Would you like to come in?"

They were taken aback by her words. "Thank you," the detective stammered. "This is the first time anyone has ever invited me in. Most people loathe us. We are, indeed, a nuisance."

Instead of entering the house, they stepped back and left us alone. Mother listened to my story, breaking in occasionally. "Thank You, God," she said. "Thank You, Lord."

As the night advanced, believers began arriving quietly, one at a time, at our home. They were all surprised to see me. Reverend Chae spoke in a loud voice.

"Sorrow has turned into joy in the castle of Susa. Queen Esther won the victory by violating the law in order to save her people." As he spoke, he repeatedly cried out, "Hallelujah." Weeping with joy, we all sang hymns and praised God. These people and many others in the mountains, the valleys, and the underground church had been fasting and praying for us.

The next night Pastor Lee came with one of the believers.

People arrived, night after night, eager to listen to my report. I had to go over the same story again and again, because they were so anxious to hear how God had worked in my life.

They dared not come to see us during the day, for the detective who evidently was in charge of me often would arrive unexpectedly. Whenever he left, I always had the uneasy feeling that another thread had been wound around my neck, binding me a little tighter than before. For that reason I secretly found a house and moved there without reporting it to the police. Days passed without our seeing a detective, and believers grew bold enough to come to see us during the daytime. But the news we heard was bleak, making the future dark. History was repeating itself. Nero's persecution had returned.

17

NATIONWIDE ARREST AND PERSECUTION

Although we were constantly being reminded of the suffering of others for their faith, our lives during that period were quiet and uneventful. Without becoming aware of it, we were beginning to relax, as though, somehow, we might be permitted to escape the sort of suffering others were experiencing. Then we were visited by an elementary teacher who had been tortured severely for her faith. After lunch she left to go back to her own home. Half an hour later she was back, ashen faced and trembling. Detective Yoo was with her. I had been instructed to give the police my new address if I moved, and I had not done so.

"You don't have to hide," he said exultantly.

From that moment, the detectives kept a close watch on our home and I knew that the time of my arrest was near.

It was three o'clock one chill autumn morning, and my mother had gone to the mountain alone to pray, as was her custom. I was kneeling in prayer myself when Detective Yoo came for me.

"Lord," I whispered to God, "the time has come."

I had had plenty of time to plan what I was going to do, but now, as I went into the bedroom and wrote a note to my mother, telling her what was happening, there was an air of unreality about it, except for the icy dread in my heart.

Quickly I put on as much underwear and as many warm clothes as possible and picked up a blanket, hoping I would be able to keep it with me. A favorite Scripture verse came to mind: "He shall call upon me, and I will answer him; I will be with him in trouble: I will deliver him, and honor him" (Psalm 91:15).

An adventurous expectation rose within me, and I hoped whimsically for a miracle. But I saw none. Although it was very early in the morning, the outer office at the Pyongyang police station was crowded with officers and Christians. The secret service division, where I was taken, also was crowded. Lesser policemen were interrogating most of the believers who had been arrested in this latest purge, but a superintendent from the capital had come to question the Christian leaders. Detective Yoo must have had orders to take me to the executive officer.

The police superintendent looked questioningly at me. "You're not making a mistake are you?" he asked my arresting officer. "Is she really Ahn Ei Sook?"

Detective Yoo assured him that I was.

"I thought Ahn Ei Sook must be either a heroic woman or headstrong," the superintendent continued. "But she is a rather lovely girl, quite different than I imagined she would be." He offered me a chair and asked me if I was, indeed, the person he was supposed to question. When I told him I was, he said, "You speak like a silver bell." He put his pen aside, and it was a long while before he spoke again. "Take her to Sun Kyori," he told the detective at last. "You don't have to do anything harsh."

My heart was as light as a swallow on the wing. I felt as if I had just thrust a spear into the chest of a wild beast that was about to attack me.

Leaving the secret service division, I saw believers who were being beaten and kicked for their faith. My heart was dark and heavy. When we reached the Sun Kyori police building, I was handed over to another police officer.

I remembered that Jesus had also experienced such things. How Jesus' heart must have ached! Compared with His suffering, how could I complain? I determined that I would accept with thanksgiving whatever difficulties might befall me.

"Why does a gracious lady like you have to go through this hardship?" the guard asked me in Korean as he took me to the detention house. "Why don't you live a more easy life? You don't have to be so strict with yourself."

"I'm fighting for my faith," I told him. "The Japanese will probably kill me, but it's more terrible for me to live against my conscience than to rebel against the nation and its laws." Then I asked him if he would go to my mother's home and tell her where I was being held.

"I certainly will, Teacher," he said.

I was placed in a cell for women in a new building, an exact copy of the Tokyo jail where I was first held. The cells, constructed of iron bars, were arranged, one beside the other, on the outside edge of the big room. The jailer was high on a platform in the center so he could see everything that went on. Since I was the only woman prisoner in that crowded jail at the time, everyone stared at me.

I sat on the floor and talked to God. My battle had finally begun. I asked Him to be with me and give me courage and to watch over all the other Christians who had been arrested in Pyongyang and were being tortured.

"Keep them in Your love," I prayed.

My determination was strong, but I knew the weakness of my own body and was uncertain about how long I could endure.

I was shocked to see that the old man with the white beard in the first cell was Reverend Lee. He had already suffered so much, and now he had been arrested again and only death awaited him. But his faith was firm, and his attitude was that of a martyr. I wept as I looked at him.

Why did the Japanese hate those who were noble and meek? Wasn't God protecting this land because of such saints as Reverend Lee? Who could do anything but mourn this age when those who loved God were hated more than murderers? As the people of Israel killed the Saviour on the cross, so were the Japanese now killing the saints. The Japanese government had gone mad.

Lunch was two pieces of salty radish and some millet mixed with sand. When it was over, many of the prisoners were taken out of their cells for inspection. They came back, soaked with sweat and suffering miserably. I could only guess how savagely they had been beaten.

I felt myself cringing in fear. One day it would happen to me. I would have to rely on God day by day to give me the strength and courage to meet whatever would come upon me. Even though it would be unspeakably hard, I would be able to experience the Lord in a deeper way and see His promises fulfilled.

I watched Reverend Lee sitting quietly and calmly in the first cell, his eyes closed in prayer. I had never once seen him impatient. I thought of the apostle John's disciple, Polycarp, who stood alone as a martyr. He must have been just such a person as Reverend Lee.

"The grass withereth," I quoted to myself from the book of Isaiah, "the flower fadeth: because the breath of Jehovah bloweth upon it; surely the people is grass. The grass withereth, the flower fadeth; but the word of our God shall stand forever" (40:7–8).

How meaningful it would be to offer this youthful life to the most beloved God!

"Jesus," I said to Him, "You know how unworthy I am. I feel ashamed for having done nothing to deserve Your noble and most beautiful sacrificial love. But with this heart and soul filled with hope, I would like to offer myself to You, even though I am worth nothing."

I thought I had practiced well in the months before my arrest, but when I lay on the floor without any bedding, the cold felt so sharp that I could not sleep. I was coughing continuously. It was now only the beginning of autumn. How terrible it would be when winter came! Softly I recited Bible verses and sang as many hymns as I could remember.

Late the next afternoon, a detective dragged in a long-haired youth who had been beaten so badly that he could scarcely walk. I was afraid he would die before the night was over.

"Why was he tortured so much?" I asked the jailer in Japanese when he came near my cell.

"He is a criminal of dangerous thoughts," he told me. "He wrote a poem called 'Tomorrow Will Come.'"

For doing that, the boy had been arrested and held for three months, suffering many such beatings. His poem spoke of the day when Japan would be defeated and our people freed, but I found a different meaning in the title of his poem. When death came, eternity would begin. Then we would see the true "tomorrow morning."

After a week I was questioned by the police superintendent, who wanted to know how I found life worth living.

"I'm beginning to understand what faith really is," I told him.

"She is ignorant of the world," one of the men told him. "That's why she can be so calm."

"She's been in school all the time," the senior officer observed, "and has been spoiled by it. The other day I confiscated her diary and read it. You can't be too careful with her."

A renewed strength surged through me as I realized how wonderfully God had been working for me. I kept my diary in Japanese, which allowed the superintendent to read it without difficulty. It was really more than a diary. I had recorded my faith in poetry and prose, my confessions and repentance before God, and he could not have found anything political in it. I had been keeping the diary for ten years, so it must have taken him a long time to read it through. At the close of the inter-view he told one of the officers to make a desk available for me and give me paper and a pen so that I could continue to write my diary.

18

HELL
ON EARTH

very day there was a change of jailers. A uniformed Korean
policeman was followed by a Japanese officer, and new
guards were brought in continually. I suspected this was
to keep us from getting too well acquainted with the jailer and
to make sure that the Japanese were constantly aware of what
was going on.

I learned other things during my long imprisonment. One
was that the jailer set the tone for the day, so it was either
pleasant or miserable for the prisoners according to his mood.

One particular Japanese police officer was cruel and sadis-
tic. A terrible wickedness marred his ugly features, and his behavior was that of a beast. His orders were profane and
completely unpredictable.

Some prisoners watched anxiously at each changing of the
jailer to see what they could expect from the new guard, but I
did not feel anxious. Every prisoner in every cell was soon
aware of this man, however. As soon as the man he had relieved was gone, he whipped off his hat and threw it in a

corner. I had never before seen a jailer, and especially a Japanese jailer, take off his hat while on duty.

Usually they obeyed every regulation to the most minute detail.

A hush fell over the cells, and hearts trembled, for a man like this could do anything. No one was there to stop him. When night came, he still would not allow us to sleep. We had to continue to sit up straight without moving, though we were all exhausted from the tension of the day. He moved from one cell to another, his bloodshot eyes fierce and flaming with anger. Someone was going to feel the force of his wrath. That much we knew.

Finally the blow fell. A prisoner was chosen for no reason at all, forced to come out of his cell, and set before the jailer on the concrete floor. With his leather belt as a whip, the jailer lashed the prisoner brutally. He was a powerful man, and each blow tore the helpless prisoner's battered flesh. The poor man cried out in agony, but his screams of pain only seemed to increase the intensity of the beating. His bloody shirt was ripped to shreds, and the concrete around him was stained crimson when he finally lost consciousness. Only then did the savage battering stop.

The jailer had enjoyed every moment. Perspiration from the beating he had administered soaked his shirt and streamed down his face. Grinning, he wiped it away with his handkerchief. "Now, that was good exercise!" he exclaimed.

Another prisoner was ordered to clean up the floor and was beaten, himself, when he didn't work fast enough to satisfy the evil jailer.

This was hell on earth. Witnessing it, I could not but praise the love of Jesus who had saved us from eternal hell.

Soon after the incident, I was called by the detective from the secret service division and told to write a report concerning my thoughts. *I will write about how the cells are like hell,* I thought.

I wrote down everything that had happened as accurately as I knew how. To the report, I added my own impressions.

> I was surprised when I learned what the Japanese police are really like. . . . A prisoner with no crime at all is judged as a far more wicked criminal than a murderer or a burglar. Most of the Christians have been beaten ruthlessly to the point of death because they want to be faithful to the law of God. . . . How long and how much will those believers have to endure from the cruelty of policemen who consider it their physical exercises to torture men? . . . I feel that I could never die until I let the world know about these facts and write them into history.

My paper was twenty pages long.

Several days later the Korean jailer told me that my report had caused the Japanese police officer to be discharged. But that wasn't all. My report was mimeographed and sent to all the police departments in the country. In the days that followed we were to see a change in the attitude of our jailers toward us. Every policeman seemed to be more careful in keeping the regulations.

It wasn't long, however, until I was taken back to the Pyongyang station and told that I was to be moved to the very quiet Soon Chon police station.

19

A DIFFERENT JAIL AND A RENEWED VOW

A s I looked out the window of the train, the autumn landscape was beautiful. Sheaves of grain were scattered about the fields to be dried by the gentle hand of the fall sun. The reds and yellows had darkened to brown in the leaves that still remained on the trees, and winter would soon arrive.

The clouds that were floating so serenely in the sky knew no agony or suffering. That was to their pity, it seemed to me. The greater the suffering for a child of God, the greater the blessing would be. Suddenly I was filled with thankfulness.

"Come agony and suffering!" my heart cried out. "I have the true God with me. He shall be manifest."

The police station to which I was being taken was in a quiet area in the country. I was immediately taken to the secret service division where the Japanese officer in charge treated me like a criminal. Instead of reading my papers, which were on his desk, he questioned me harshly.

As he did so, my heart was darkened and heavy. Where had the bold resolution gone that I had made on the train? He was still questioning me when the chief policeman sent for him. In about ten minutes I was taken to the chief's office. The chief's face was ugly and wrinkled, and he walked with the painful limp of an old man. He gave me the impression that he was as vulgar and as arrogant as the detective who had been questioning me. However, he was courteous and respectful. I couldn't understand why until he told me that he had received a phone call from the prefectural government, instructing him to have me write a paper concerning my thoughts. God had gone ahead of me and prepared the way.

The kindly behavior of the chief policeman seemed very funny to me. I felt like laughing, especially when the chief ordered one of the janitors to go to the cell and clean it well. But I dared not laugh. I will never know what might have happened if I had showed any mirth on my face.

Only four cells were in the country jail where I was being held, and I only saw two or three prisoners. The jailer acted as though he didn't even see me until we were alone. Then he wanted to know why I was being held in jail. I told him that I was a criminal because of dangerous thoughts. When he found out I had gone to high school, he wanted to know what kind of crime I had committed.

"I am a Christian," I told him. "I have been brought here because I refused to worship the shrine."

"You fool!" he exclaimed. "What are you becoming by doing such a thing?"

The next day the department head called me out and questioned me arrogantly. I told him about our complicated family life, that my father took several concubines because my mother did not have a son, and that there were boys and girls born to him every year. I told him how my grandmother worshiped idols and invited soothsayers and sorceresses to the house all the time.

"Through them I saw that idols and demons are unable to do any good for their worshipers," I said. "I knew how unhappy and powerless my grandmother was. But my mother, who was saved by Jesus Christ and believed in the true God, Jehovah, was the happiest person, and she was living a life of peace and victory in spite of the fact that she was in a most miserable situation. I did not become a Christian because somebody told me to do so and taught me about God. Rather, I made up my mind and believed after seeing the facts with my own eyes."

I told him about our trip to Japan to warn the leaders and how I had accompanied the man who dropped the bill of warning.

"I believe that the Japanese police will treat me badly until I die, and that I will be sentenced to death in the end," I continued.

At first he took notes, but he soon stopped and only listened to me. His entire attitude changed as I kept on talking, and from time to time he offered me some tea. When I told him about the violent jailer at the Sun Kyori police station, his eyes widened.

"The admonition was given here, too!" he explained. "So it was you!"

He stood quickly and got out his lunch box, offering it to me.

"I'm starving," I admitted.

"I don't blame you," he said. "You didn't eat anything yesterday." I finished eating the food without any hesitation. What a shameful thing! And how shy I felt! But at the same time I was glad. Having eaten and laughed to my heart's content, I was as serene as the high autumn sky. I pictured the smiling face of Jesus, and within myself I praised the love of God.

Then the chief policeman called me to his room, asked the department head to leave, and began to make trivial gossip. When he saw that did not please me, he quit.

"You seem to have a clear mind for a woman," he said.

I looked at him without answering.

"Don't you know that a sweet woman is more charming than a smart one?" he asked, seeming to be offended that my education exceeded his own. "Do you want to go with me to see Ki Ko Rang sing 'The Night in China' in this town tonight?"

I glanced at him in surprise. However, I was not that foolish as to agree. I looked back at him coldly.

"What are you thinking of?" he asked.

"I'm thinking of writing down my thoughts in a report," I replied.

He didn't like to hear that.

"I will have to remember to write down everything that has happened," I continued.

"How foolish!" he exclaimed. "Who in the world could remember everything and write it down? Forget it!"

I was taken back to my cell immediately.

The following morning the department head came earlier than usual and took me to the secret service division. He seemed concerned about me and ordered me a warm breakfast. Then he picked up my Japanese Bible and asked if he could look at it. I prayed earnestly that he might be saved by the Holy Spirit just by reading the portions underlined in red.

During the next several days, news about me must have spread. One by one the police officers came by to have a look at me. On one occasion the chief policeman came to my cell and told the jailer to lock the door of my cell only at night and to let me go in and out freely during the day. From that time on, I would put on my shoes and go up the hill in the back of the building to watch the sky, to sing, to recite Scripture, or to pray. At times a policeman would follow me, so I was careful not to go too far. In order that they would not have to come out and look for me, I spent the day where they could see me from the office window.

I realized anew that there was one part of creation of which I was especially mindful. It was man. Each person could gladden or sadden the heart of God. Among all the creatures, God had created human beings the most carefully and had breathed His own Spirit into them. And I was one of them.

What an honor and privilege! As I thought about the mind of God, who must have been looking down at me, my heart was filled with thankfulness, and I determined anew to live in faith until the end.

"Lord," I promised, "I shall obey."

20

A CHANGE
OF HEART

When Mother came to see me she brought disturbing news. The believers who were detained at Pyongyang were being tortured viciously, and their families were meeting in secret to fast and pray for them.

"Lord," I prayed tearfully, "show me what I can do. Use me to help the persecuted saints."

During the night I went to the chief's room and asked for paper and a pen. I wrote:

DEAR POLICE SUPERINTENDENT RUGA:

 I want to thank you for your kindness in having me moved to Soon Chon Police Station. However, isn't it illegal to have me detained without any examination? Anyone who is detained ought to be given a trial to determine whether he is innocent or guilty. I have done the same things as those Christian leaders who are being detained at the Pyongyang Police Station. I am no different than they. Shouldn't I also be tried? If you keep me here, perhaps it might cause some kind of danger.

I added the last puzzling hint of danger to attract his attention. As I had suspected, the third day after the letter was written, he came to see me, bringing a police inspector with him. He was in good spirits and seemed glad to see me.

"What did you mean when you wrote about some kind of danger?" he asked.

I did not answer him. Actually, I had written irresponsibly, for I wanted to be taken to Pyongyang as soon as possible.

"Mr. Superintendent," the head jailer said nervously, as though he were somehow at fault, "I suppose she has something she could not say in words since she is so young and pretty. You know, there are many single men in this station." He talked as if he actually believed what he was saying.

"That old man [the chief] is quite a character, too, isn't he?" the police inspector said.

Apparently the chief had a bad reputation. I neither confirmed nor denied their speculation.

"That is dangerous," Superintendent Kuga said. "It was my fault that I didn't know it." Still, he hesitated. "Pyongyang is so dirty, one could suffocate there."

"I'm a criminal," I reminded him. "Don't you think it's natural that a criminal should go to a dirty and awful place?"

Before he left, the superintendent indicated that I might be transferred back to Pyongyang, but he did not make any promises. Finding this disturbing, I prayed morning and night that I would be sent to Pyongyang. During that period, the head jailer called me into his office and offered me a chair.

"Miss Ahn," he said, "I have decided to resign and go back to Japan."

I was astonished by what he said, but there was clear determination on his face. "You're going to resign?"

"I want to start a new life."

Thinking that he might have been discharged, I was disturbed. "I've come to loathe my job," he said. "Officially, I am leaving for a rest, but a change has come to my heart. I want to live for a rewarding and true hope as you are doing."

I was speechless.

He took the Japanese Bible he had borrowed from me and asked if I would give it to him. Of course I would. It was just like the Bible I gave to General Ugaki, I told him.

"I have prayed for you a lot," I said.

"You've prayed for me? Now I understand."

He took me to the hill in back and expressed his concern that I might catch cold in the coming winter. I only nodded to him. I was so moved I could speak no words. In my heart I knelt beside the feet of Jesus, overjoyed to see such a miraculous spiritual change in a police station which was, so to speak, a human zoo.

Although I did not see him again, I constantly prayed that he would also receive the faith I had been given while I read my Bible.

Many weeks passed without any news about my request, and then one midnight a detective and a uniformed policeman came to my cell, handcuffed me, and moved me to the Pyongyang police station.

Arriving in Pyongyang, we were getting off the train when I heard a young woman cry out my name. Thinking of the possible danger for her since I was with policemen, I walked swiftly away without even looking in the direction of her voice. My heart was hurrying to the Pyongyang police station.

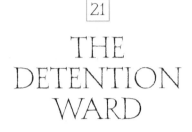

THE
DETENTION
WARD

At the Pyongyang police station I was taken to the detention ward in the basement

"I don't know why you hated that quiet Soon Chon police station and wanted to come here," the officer who was escorting me said, "but you asked for it, so don't complain."

A terrible smell slammed into my face as he opened the door. It choked off my breathing and burned into my eyes. My stomach revolted, and for a moment I thought I would be sick.

The building was old, and the cells that stretched endlessly on either side of the cement corridor were made of logs. The prisoners had their eyes closed, as though in sleep. The cells were so overcrowded that there was not space for everyone to lie down, so some were sitting, their arms wrapped around their knees.

A red light was shining dimly on the faces of the prisoners, but it was so weak that I could not distinguish individuals. I grew impatient, anxious to let the believers know I had joined them.

"I am Ahn Ei Sook!" I called out loudly. "I have moved here from Soon Chon station."

A clatter went up among the prisoners, and the jailer struggled vainly to quiet them. *Hallelujah!* my heart shouted. Now the believers knew that I was with them.

I was put into number eight cell. It was just like a pigpen.

Soon a prisoner in the cell across from me got to his feet and cautiously bowed to me. I wasn't sure, but I thought I recognized him. In return, I bowed deeply to him. Since the jailer was still close, we only watched each other in silence. When the guard had gone, we talked by inscribing large characters in the air with an outstretched finger.

"I am Reverend Joo," he told me.

Praise God! As soon as I had come to this place the Lord had made it possible for me to meet this great saint.

As we used our hands to talk with each other, I continued to watch his face. He must have been tortured beyond description, but the expression on his face was serene. He told me which cells other Christian leaders were being held in, and asked why I had wanted to come to such a place.

I told him that I only knew I had to come. Then the jailer came back and we feigned sleep.

Three female prisoners were in my cell. The odor from the toilets and unwashed bodies was so offensive that I pinched my nose with my fingers and closed my mouth tightly, trying not to breathe.

"In a week or so," one of the other women said, "you'll get used to it."

I was ashamed to think of what Reverend Joo or the other believers would think if they had seen me. Even worse, I was ashamed to think of Jesus' attitude toward me. He had left His glorious throne as the only Son of God in order to be born into this world of sin, evil, and rebellion. What shame and humiliation that must have been! And what a tremendous sacrifice it had been for Him to live here on earth and to die on the cross as a human being for the sake of us sinners. Why was such a sinful, worthless one as myself complaining about the odor and filthiness of man? How awful it was to be complaining!

I opened my nose and breathed deeply. Finally I felt that I could manage without fainting. Since it was not cold, my coughing was not as bad as before, and I was able to sleep till morning.

The next day we were served the familiar two pieces of radish and the yellowish, starchless millet mixed with sand.

"Eat this and fight well," I said to myself. I swallowed it like everyone else was doing. Because of the sand we were unable to chew.

Shortly after breakfast I was taken to the high police division. "Well, you did not suffocate," a familiar voice said. "That's good."

I saw the vice head of the division standing before me. We had met a number of times before.

The office I was in was on the east side of the building, and the morning sunshine and fresh air streamed in. How refreshing! For the first time I was thankful for fresh air, something among all the things that God has given us so freely.

I was given a book in Korean and told to translate it into Japanese. The vice head brought in a young police officer and charged him with the responsibility of guarding me.

"He is a novice, a chick," the head told me jokingly. "He has just graduated from junior high school and knows nothing of the world."

I asked to go back to my cell, but he refused me permission, saying he would be sentenced to death if I were confined there and suffocated. As soon as he was gone, I picked up the book and started to read. My guard also picked up a book, but that didn't hold his attention long. He left me alone and went to the business office where some of his friends were working. He was back in a little while and picked up his book again.

"If you keep on reading," I chided him, "I might escape. You should keep your eyes open wide."

"If you escape," he said calmly, "I'll escape, too."

"If you let me escape," I insisted, "you'll be a condemned criminal."

But that did not disturb him. "If you flee, Major General Hibiki will give me a decoration."

I was surprised. How could this boy know about the Major General and myself? I asked him.

"Major General Hibiki and Congressman Matsuyama came here to the station. They came to see you." He went on to tell me that they had been on their way to attend a conference in Nanking and dropped in without any previous notice. "You were at Soon Chon," he continued, "and there wasn't time to bring you here. But they were talking about you!"

I could scarcely believe it. It filled me with joy and thanks to God to know that He had been working so hard to make things as good as possible for His believers, even for such a sinner as myself.

The young officer told me other things. An order had been circulated throughout all Korea to arrest the Christian leaders. On an early September morning, all the known Christians throughout Korea were detained simultaneously, and their torture was more ruthless than ever before. "They want to wipe out Christianity in one massive action," he said. "As a result, the physical beatings by the policemen were extremely severe.

About the same time, the Manchurian flu was raging throughout Korea. A savage, virulent strain that often brought death, it spread fast among the policemen. And, strangely, it seemed to attack the detectives who were in charge of torturing the believers. More than half of the police department employees were absent from work for a while, and four particularly merciless officers died. The policemen began to worry that they might die next. From then on, no police officer was willing to torture the believers, and the persecution seemed to be less severe.

Police Superintendent Kuga, who was the general commander in charge of this phase of Christian persecution, was singled out for trouble. When the husband of his only daughter was shot in the head in battle, he was returned to the Kuga home to stay, but he was in such tremendous pain that he could not sit or sleep. The pain was so savage that he cried constantly and had fits of groaning and screaming and jumping up and down like someone who is losing his mind. His pain was strikingly similar to that of some of Kuga's victims who were tortured for their faith.

But that was not all. Next his daughter fell victim to the flu, and the high fever infected her bones until they became like jelly. She was placed in a cast and had to lie flat on her back, unable even to feed herself.

God had not forsaken those believers who had suffered so greatly. It was indeed a miracle, an extraordinary work of God.

When I was taken back to my cell, Reverend Joo had been awaiting my return. Writing in the air with my fingers, I told him everything.

"Now let's pray that the policemen, starting with Superintendent Kuga, will repent and be saved. I believe your task is also for this purpose."

Since I thought he must be exhausted by this time, I decided to sleep, too. This was my home. Why not sleep happily and peacefully, breathing the same air the saints were breathing, and sleeping on the same floor on which they were sleeping. I was going to live each day and each hour joyfully, creating fun and being happy that everything was a plan from God.

One day as I was working on the translation, a Korean detective came in. He was so fat, like a pig. I hated even to see his face, thinking he might have been the one who tortured my friends.

"I wish I could leave this difficult job and become a prisoner like you," he said seriously. Then he lowered his voice. "If you have anything you want to do, I'll gladly do it for you. There are two good jailers in the ward: Saito, the Japanese, and Che, a Korean."

I knew them both.

"If you ask them for anything, they will do it. Late at night, ask for meat buns. They will buy them and bring them to you."

What he said was true, my heart told me. Those two seemed to be sensible. They were not profane and looked honest and compassionate.

That very night I let Reverend Joo know what I had learned. I could not wait for Jailer Che to come on duty. When he did, I asked him for a pencil. He wanted to know what I was going to use it for. In a few minutes he brought me a pen and a piece of paper. "You won't make trouble, will you?" he asked me.

I wrote him a short message, telling him that the Christian leaders in the ward were innocent and very, very hungry. I asked him to take money from my purse and purchase meat buns for them.

He read the message and burned it without saying anything. I didn't know whether he would help us or not, but very late at night he shook me awake and handed me a bag of meat buns through the lattice. I shared my buns with the two new women prisoners in my cell, who were awakened by the smell of food. Looking across the corridor, I could see that Reverend Joo was also eating.

At his next turn around the ward, the jailer told me that he had only been able to give food to prisoners in two cells. Two days later he would try again. "But I have to be extremely careful," he said. "There are some vicious criminals in some of the cells."

I was deeply moved. God had provided an angel to minister to us through the kindly jailer.

One day while I was in the special police division working at the translation of a book into Japanese, Superintendent Kuga and a police inspector went into a nearby conference room.

"They have asked Detective Bak to help them question Reverend Chae," the janitor told me.

That bit of news was particularly disturbing. Pastor Chae was an old man, as frail as a march reed, and he had been brutally tortured. As quietly as possible, I got to my feet and went to the conference room door.

I could hear the harsh arrogance in the voice of the interrogator, and the sharp crack of the lash as it bit into the helpless old pastor's flesh. "Speak up!" the detective ordered. "Don't pretend to be ignorant of what you, yourself, told me!"

The whip came down again. I could control myself no longer. My heart was aflame, and all my blood rushed to my head. I jerked open the door and dashed into the conference room!

Pastor Chae was in the center of the room, so exhausted from the beating that he could not even sit erect. His poor, battered body was torn and bleeding. My sudden appearance stunned the three police officers. They stared at me numbly. Several pieces of firewood were at the feet of the detective who was conducting the questioning. I knew he was so infuriated at being unable to force Reverend Chae to talk that he would soon be using the pieces of wood as clubs on the tortured old man. I picked up the firewood and threw it out the window so quickly that the men could only stare at me.

"How could you do such a thing?" the detective asked numbly.

I whirled on him in anger at what he had been doing.

"I'll be beaten in his place," I said. "I'm a TB patient anyway, so I'll die very quickly if I'm beaten. Go ahead! Beat me as much as you want, but leave him alone!"

He was furious at me and his face reflected his anger, but for some reason he said nothing.

"It doesn't make any difference how hard you beat Pastor Chae, you will get no information from his mouth," I went on. "There is only love for God and for the people in his heart! How would you like to be beaten so ruthlessly when you get older? Go home and beat your father with firewood!"

Tears flooded my eyes, rolled down my face, and fell to the floor.

The detective seemed to cower as a dog who had been kicked by his master. He sighed deeply but could not speak.

At that moment Superintendent Kuga again took charge of the situation.

"That's all!" he ordered. "Take this old man to his cell!"

Like the lions who would have torn Daniel's body apart, the Japanese officials were miraculously tightly bound in the use of their power. They had the power to destroy Reverend Chae, but they could not use it. What a marvelous God we have!

Later, after reporting everything that had happened to Reverend Joo, I asked him what he would first like to do if he were to be released.

"I would love to stand in the pulpit and give a beautiful sermon on the Gospel." There was a long pause. "Before I die," he went on, "I want to present a sermon into which I can pour all my flesh and blood."

I could not stop my tears from flowing. I prayed that God would allow this loyal saint to fulfill his dream.

On another occasion I asked him what he would like to eat the most.

"A dish of spring greens," he said. "I wish I could eat them to my heart's content."

"I believe that plenty of spring greens will be served to you very soon." I thought I understood what he meant but could not be sure.

"I wish so, too," he said.

My heart was unable to rest. While I was working at the special police division, I waited longingly for Superintendent Kuga. When he went into the office of one of the men, I went in to see him. He joked with me when I told him I had a favor to ask of him, but his gentle expression encouraged me to continue. I asked him to allow the pastors to have some food brought to them from their homes.

"The millet meal is sandy and doesn't even half fill such a tiny box as this," I told him. "And only two pieces of bitter, salty radish are added."

When that seemed to have no effect on him, I asked him if I should bring a prisoner's meal to him. "So you, too, can taste it," I told him.

Several days later when I was talking to Reverend Joo with my finger, I told him I wanted to laugh loudly.

"You can find things to laugh about in such a place?" he asked.

"Seeing the proud faces of the high officials at the special police division makes me want to burst out laughing. Doesn't the Bible say that the nations and peoples who worship idols will surely perish? Japan will surely perish. Right? To think of what will become of those proud big shots makes me feel so funny that I cannot help laughing."

"No one can ever catch up with your faith," he wrote back to me. "To think that you can see such a thing when everyone is trembling under cruel persecution!"

We were still talking when two detectives came in and took three of the Christian leaders, including Reverend Joo. A little later when I was taken up to work, I saw those three saints of God. They had changed into new, clean white clothes and were eating all sorts of delicious foods. I looked particularly at Reverend Joo's plate. He was eagerly eating a dishful of spring greens!

After that, a change in regulations permitted a few families at a time to visit their jailed relatives, bringing a change of clothes and food.

Like many others, Reverend Joo asked me why I was single. I told him God had forbidden me to marry. I had seriously considered getting married when I was in Japan and met a young and respectable Japanese friend of my uncle.

"If you marry a Japanese and become an idol worshiper," Mother had told me, "you will become my enemy."

When she said that, I gave up all my plans and, after graduating from college, returned home to teach at a girls' high school.

Mother wanted me to marry a pastor, and she began to pray for the man I would marry, I told Pastor Joo.

"One morning I dashed out and knelt down beside her," I said, "praying in a loud voice, 'Lord, don't listen to my mother's prayer. Close Your ears just this time. Ignore her prayer.'

"I felt that I was not worthy to become a pastor's wife. I wanted to marry a civil engineer."

"So, what was the result?" the elderly pastor asked.

"No civil engineer showed up, nor was a suitable pastor found for me. Now everything has passed, and I am satisfied in being able to die without becoming a pastor's wife."

"Do you think a pastor is so miserable?"

"I think he is a slave," I said, "with hands, legs, mouth, and even his own will completely bound."

"Your prayer that your mother's prayers might not be heard shows how close your fellowship is with God," he said. "It shows how beautifully faith lives in your life."

"I was desperate," I told him. "Everything my mother prayed for would turn out just as she prayed."

22

A YOUNG
REBEL

One day as I was translating, a young prisoner was brought to my desk and directed to sit across from me. He was introduced as the leader of the Communist party in our section of Korea.

"Ju is like ice inside," I was told, "but he speaks excellent Japanese and has an education as fine as yours."

I stared at him. I had never met a Communist before. He did not cringe under my stare but met my gaze openly. His young body was thin and emaciated and his complexion was yellow, indicating he had not been in the sun for a long while. His hair and beard were long and unkempt.

"Why don't you talk about something?" the police head asked. "Ju is such a coldhearted Communist that I thought he might melt and warm up a little if he talked with Miss Ahn."

"I would, indeed, wish to become warmer," he said.

I asked him if he were truly a Communist. He seemed staggered and glanced at the police officer quickly.

"I am a hot, burning Christian," I told him. "I truly believe in Jesus and am proud of being a Christian."

Once again I asked if he was being detained because he was working for Communism. "Why don't you just tell us that you are a Communist?" I persisted.

He was stunned by what I said and kept watching me. The police head only grinned and listened. I realized, then, that Ju wasn't able to speak frankly because he had not confessed that he was a Communist.

I wanted to share Christ with him but didn't know how to explain, so I asked him again if he had ever read the Bible. He said that he hadn't.

"Do you want to read it?" I asked.

"I wouldn't mind."

I asked the police head to give him my Bible which he had been keeping. Ju took it awkwardly and began to fumble with the pages. "Would you like to read it all the way through?"

He hesitated. "Will you answer my questions after I read it?"

I assured him I would and told him it would probably take him three weeks or so to read it all.

"I'll read it within a week," he promised.

Aware that he was hungry, I asked the supervisor if I could order him lunch. Ju ordered six servings. While he was waiting for it, the supervisor began to tease him. Then the officer directed his attention to me.

"You are a great woman," he said, keeping his voice low. "The other prisoners who come here are like mice before cats, but you look as if you were a queen leading a fleet of chariots."

"If I am a queen, why do I have to suffer such oppression and humiliation?" I asked him.

"Aren't the policemen like your best friends or servants?" he asked.

"That's right," the police head broke in. "You have eyes to see. We are all like your servants."

Ju wanted to know if he would have been treated as well if he were a woman.

"Who would treat a Communist woman well?" the supervisor retorted. "Don't you realize? God is protecting this young lady. She is different from you knaves. That's why she told you to read the Bible."

I knew he was joking, but still I was astounded. How true his explanation was!

Again Ju assured me that he would read the Bible through in a week and would be back to ask questions. Then he told me that he was in the same cell with Pastor Joo.

"I have seen all that you've been doing," he said proudly. I surmised that he intended his words as a threat.

"I never dreamed there was someone in his cell who was watching me," I retorted firmly.

"I wish such a famous saint as Reverend Joo and a Communist chief like Ju would talk things over and have peace between each other. Do you ever talk with him?" the supervisor asked.

"Isn't there a regulation that prisoners should never talk with each other?" Ju inquired.

"That's right."

Lunch was delivered, and Ju could scarcely wait until the dishes were served. One after another he ate all the six servings of *sushi* and noodles. I was so astounded that I even forgot to eat my own food. When I asked him if he wanted some more, he said he would eat it if it were given to him. So I gave him my lunch.

I knew I shouldn't question the police head about the young man, but I did ask him how long Ju would be imprisoned if he were found guilty.

"For life," he said. "He will have to starve to death in a damp, dark cell."

A week later when I returned from my work at the special police division I was about to enter my cell when I heard someone whisper to me. It was Ju, who was sitting very close to Reverend Joo. He raised his hand high and started to write in the air.

"I have finished reading the Bible. I could not read it

through in a week, but I did finish it in eight days. Now, let me ask you questions.

"What would you like to ask?"

"I have heard that God is loving and will forgive anyone who sins, but when I read the Bible it says God will punish those who commit sins."

Then he went on. "If Jesus had been the Son of God, why didn't He come down from the cross?"

I thought I could read Ju's heart. Wasn't this the voice of those who hated and rejected the Son of God that day?

Although the young man had read the Bible so diligently, he was unable to see the truth itself that was so clearly manifested in it.

23

INQUISITION

Police superintentent Kuga came to the Pyongyang police station to conduct my examination himself. He joked about it at first, but he was very serious when he launched the official questioning.

"Aren't you plotting to become a leader of the Korean Independence Movement?" he asked, staring coldly at me. "Aren't you gathering these old pastors and jobless young men to train them spiritually, planting anti-Japan thoughts in them so you can lead them into organized action?"

He was so serious and the charge was so ridiculous that I had difficulty in refraining from laughter. "What have I to do with independence or leadership?" I asked him. "I'm a believer in the Gospel, which is a declaration of God's love. It teaches about sin and salvation. I was saved from sin by Jesus, and for this reason I am determined not to rebel against Him, even to the extent of risking my life. If I have any other purpose, it will only prove the failure of my faith and then my death will become meaningless."

He repeated his question, his tone even more serious and stern than before.

"If you want to believe that, you may go ahead," I answered coldly.

"What is your opinion of the shrine worship?" he inquired.

I did not hesitate in my answer. "Worshiping the shrine is idolatry and it is a breaking of the first and second commandments of God."

"If the state regulates that its people must worship the shrine," he persisted, "don't the people have to worship, even if it is an idol?"

"God clearly forbids us to do so." I knew I was on dangerous ground, but I could say nothing less. "I shall never break His commandment, even if I might be killed for it. Because His commandments reveal His love for us, I can't offend God. The law of God stands above the law of any state. If a state's laws violate God's law, that state cannot be maintained. Throughout the history of mankind, we have learned that many powerful nations have ceased to exist because of this."

"You mean that Japan will perish?"

"Yes, indeed. The clearest evidence that Japan rebels against God is the fact that she puts her idols above God and persecutes the faithful servants of God as if they were criminals. Can we think that God will forsake his children when they are beaten and kicked and tortured to death? I went to Tokyo to tell the high government officials what is happening here to Christians. As I am already dead, there is nothing that I should fear."

The superintendent was listening intently to everything I had to say, and the inspector was vigorously writing it down. I felt very pleasant, as if I were singing a song.

The exchange between us continued as he defended Japan and her stand on shrine worship, boasting of the power of that great nation and the fact that she had built shrines throughout Manchuria and China as well as in Korea. And it would not be long, he assured me, until they were spread throughout all of Asia.

I told him about the ardent Christians I knew in Japan. There was Major General Hibiki, sole living general of the Russo-Japanese War and a highly respected retired officer. There were Congressman Matsuyama and former Deputy General Ugaki as well as a number of the leading professors at Tokyo Imperial University and Kyoto Imperial University.

Anger was written on Superintendent Kuga's face. I was excited. If I should be sentenced to death for this, it would mean that the task of my life was accomplished. I had only to speak boldly, calmly, freely, and clearly, as Jesus would have done.

"Do you mean that our emperor, who is a living god, must also believe in Jesus?"

"Yes. Unless the emperor, who is just a man like we are, is saved by Jesus, he will go to hell when he dies."

"That," he shouted, trembling in his anger, "is an unpardonable blasphemy!"

I remained silent.

"You are saying that you would not worship our emperor who is our living god?"

"As his subject, I would bow to him. If he were right in front of me or if he were passing by me or if I even saw him in the distance, I would bow to him as deeply as I could," I explained. "But if I am commanded to bow to him as the living God, I cannot do that. It would be idol worship."

Rage crept into his cheeks and caused his lips to tremble. I must confess to becoming worried, too, but I had to speak the truth. I would not do anything which I might forever regret. I had to please God before my death.

I asked Superintendent Kuga not to become upset about my answers, but to have the inspector write down clearly what I was saying so it could be sent to the court.

He lit a cigarette and stopped questioning me for a moment or two.

"You seem to have been made fearless," he said. "You must know what result your words will bring to you."

He soon stopped the questioning and I was taken back to my cell. The filthy cell and floor with the putrid air seemed to be only a waiting room for heaven, and my heart danced with joy. I was happy and content.

The following day the questioning was resumed. It seemed as though the superintendent wanted to have some specific crimes to charge me with. I was well aware of that, but I longed for him to continue the questioning. Actually, I was happy to see him.

"I thought you must have been deeply regretful for what you had said to me," he said, "but you look like a rose that has blossomed after the rain. Why?"

"I am happy and content."

He could not understand that, and he repeated the words questioningly.

"I have finally found the worth of having been born," I told him. "I have experienced the greatest satisfaction and happiness of my life."

His anger sparked. "Don't make me confused," he retorted.

He continued the duel of ideas with me, pointing to the glory of Japan and the ancient roots of her faith. I repeated the Word of God, speaking of the Flood and the second coming of Jesus Christ. He laughed when I told him that those who do not believe in Jesus Christ and who worship idols would fall into hell when they die. The inspector laughed too.

"Then you are saying that our emperor, the living god, will also fall into hell, for he, himself, worships the shrine?"

"Yes," I answered plainly.

"Do you know what misfortune is going to befall you for what you are saying?"

"Yes, of course. But I can't tell a lie, for Jesus Himself never tells a lie."

He sighed deeply. "I'll quit."

As far as he was concerned, that ended the examination.

I glanced up at the sky through the window, and as I looked to the face of the Lord, I opened my heart and sang.

One verse came to mind: "Who will bring a charge against God's elect? God is the one who justifies" (Romans 8:33 NASB).

24

PYONGYANG PRISON

I shall never forget the morning of September 20, 1940. That was the day that I was taken with Pastor Chae, Pastor Joo, and thirty-one other saints to Pyongyang prison. Our families, who had been told about the transfer, were waiting for us when we were taken to the special police division offices.

I saw Mother, her soft eyes awash with grief. I looked from her sad face to Pastor Chae. With his wool white hair, his kindly face and sparkling eyes, I was sure he must look something like the apostle Peter. And he had that same fierce determination of spirit that set the apostle apart.

Although I was looking forward expectantly to my fate, I couldn't help thinking what a day it was for Korean Christians. For a year the Japanese had starved and tortured the most loyal Korean Christian leaders in a ruthless attempt to stamp out their faith in Jesus Christ. Now those leaders, and myself among them, were to be executed. As one of the victims of the persecution, I would sing forever that I had been born and had lived for this purpose.

Unless a grain of wheat falls into the earth and dies, it remains by itself alone; but if it dies, it bears much fruit. He who loves his life loses it; and he who hates his life in this world shall keep it to life eternal (John 12:24–25 NASB).

I believed that the Japanese and their idols would eternally perish from this earth, just as the Lord had promised, and that the churches of Christ would be built throughout the land. Hymns praising the Lord would be heard and proclaimed throughout the mountains, valleys, and towns. The few grains that were these believers' lives would fall into the earth, die, and bear much fruit.

I could see from the convulsions on my mother's forehead that she was very tense. I was sure that she was worrying over me and the fact that I was weak and vulnerable to the cold. I spoke loudly, assuring her that I would be all right.

"You are going to die for certain this time," she said from the depths of her heart. "Look up to the gates of heaven. There we will meet."

Suddenly I envisioned a prison, one that I had passed some time before: a tall wall of red bricks stretched on endlessly. I remembered clearly how I trembled as I thought of those who lived in that horrible, suffocating place. Now I was going to be cast into that prison forever.

Even though I walk through the valley of the shadow of death, I fear no evil; for Thou art with me; Thy rod and Thy staff, they comfort me (Psalm 23:4 NASB).

Yes, the Lord would walk with me, and I would have no fear of evil. The Lord would comfort me. I would have no bitterness.

I remembered a dream in which I was on a swing. As I looked around, a great war was being waged, and numerous devils were searching for me. They were shouting and calling my name, but they would not look up at me sitting above them on the swing. They were only looking around on the earth.

"This way!" I called out to them mischievously. "On the swing! Can't you see me?"

"We hear her voice," they said to each other, "but where can she be?"

I looked up, hoping to see the pole my swing was suspended from, but it was not suspended from anything. It reached upward farther than I could see. When I woke up, I was filled with joy. No matter how hard the devils searched, they could not find me. Even though they heard my voice, they could not look up where I was.

I now realized that the more dangerous my situation became, the closer God would be to me. The harsher my torture, the more the Lord would comfort me. Up to this moment I had believed in the Lord with all my heart. Now the time had come for me to experience the work of faith. I was now to see the promises of the Lord become mine. He would care for me.

The will to know my own faith and to prove God's promises made my heart light and joyous. The Japanese would not throw us in boiling oil, or have lions eat us, or kill us with saws as the Romans killed the Christians in the first century. Rumor said that we would be hanged. That would be easier and faster than some of the other methods of execution. I was concerned about the cold, but this, too, I would have to entrust to God. Most heartbreaking to me was my mother. I knew how she would suffer and worry because of me. Bowing my head, I committed her into the hands of the Lord.

By this time the car had arrived to take us to the prison. I kept looking at the faces of the believers who were being transferred to the prison with me. They all looked happy. Even the detectives appeared gentle and did not talk to one another. It seemed as though they were our friends.

I had no idea of how many days of misery I would meet as a prisoner, but I knew that death was the only way I would be free. My heart's desire was about to come true.

Ever since I was a child, I had never had the confidence to live in this world. The world was too strong for me to cope with. Had it not been a sin against God to end one's life, I would long ago have killed myself. I wished to die while I was still young and pretty. Mother knew me well and at the time of my illness, she had always sympathized with me and prayed for me.

"Lord, take this child to heaven before You take me," she prayed. "Who will take care of her if I died? She is too weak to continue living."

My sister was the same. "You must die before I do," she told me on one occasion. "You'll be safer that way."

Once I dreamed that one tiny bug was being eaten by a large spider. Having lost all its legs, the tiny bug was about to die, yet it was struggling to live. Watching the helpless bug made me feel so miserable that sweat covered my body.

"While a wounded bug struggles to live, why do you think only of dying?" a voice asked me.

My longing to die, which almost became a part of my life, must have reached God. But I thought that God had rejected it and, instead, He had taught me to live. Still, everything in this world was frightening to me. I was afraid of those who told lies and those who talked too loudly. I was frightened to see people in poverty, and seeing sick people made me feel as though their agony would become mine. I even ran away from people who quarreled. Yet, being such a person as I was now, I could calmly prepare to die. The peace I felt had to come from God's love.

Our families had gone on ahead and were waiting for us when our car stopped before the prison and we got out. My mother was calm now, and she was more radiant than I had ever seen her. I ran to her and held both of her hands.

"Now I'm going to enter the advanced course in the college of faith," I told her. "Christ Himself is the Principal, so I am sure He will teach me about true faith. Isn't that wonderful?"

"You must follow Him completely," she said, "if you are to learn from Him. You must lose your life so that Jesus may live within you. That will mean death to yourself every day, every hour, and every minute."

Finally she seemed contented. I bowed my last bow of reverence to her, deeply.

"Let's meet at the gate of heaven," she said impulsively. "Whichever one gets there first, she shall wait there for the other."

Again and again I bowed to her.

The jailers in the prison were even more businesslike than those we had known at the police station. I was taken to the women's ward by a female jailer. It was quite far from the place where the men were held, but both sections were within the same enclosure.

Processing did not take long, and after a meticulous examination of my body, including my mouth and hair, I was given a uniform with a number. From now on I would not have a name but would be Number 57.

I was somewhat surprised to see that the prison was cleaner than the detention ward from where I had come. And I was the only prisoner in my cell.

"Lord," I prayed, closing my eyes, "at last I'm confined in such a place as this. The rest of the world has completely disappeared from me. I am a weakling. Unless I live each day holding Your hand, I'll become too frightened. Lord, hold my hand firmly so I won't part from You. Jesus, I love You."

My heart was overwhelmed by my desire to love God more. What an honorable thing to love God and to be faithful unto the end in His love! Once again I prayed.

"Instead of twelve years of imprisonment like John Bunyan, who wrote *Pilgrim's Progress,* let me be brought to the gate of heaven after six years because I am a woman."

The female jailer yelled at the prisoners and scolded them all day long, but it seemed to have little effect on them. I was fearful that she would become angry and do something cruel unless the prisoners did as she ordered. Tensely I studied her face. She saw that I was looking at her and came over and introduced herself.

"I am Ahn," I said.

"I know Number 57 well," she told me. "You need not explain anything to me."

"But this is my first imprisonment," I countered. "How could you know of me?"

"I prepared this cell for you. Besides, every female prisoner who has come here from the Pyongyang police department has been talking about you."

I was even more surprised to learn that the male prisoners had been talking about me, too.

"The jailers in the male ward have been asking me if that famous lady had come yet," the guard said.

"There's nothing famous about me," I told her.

She went on to tell me that the prisoners and other jailers made a fool of her. The prisoners knew she couldn't do cruel things to them, so they refused to obey her. I asked about the other jailers and she told me what I feared.

"They treat the prisoners badly," she said.

After she talked with me, she yelled loudly at the prisoners again. They quieted down, but only for a moment. While observing her, I felt that this prison was not the place for her. She seemed to have a tender heart.

Then her day's work was over and another jailer came on duty. The noise stopped and silence prevailed. Glancing into her face, I saw the reason. She was cruel and malicious. I sat very straight and remained silent.

LIFE IN PRISON

Jailer Kuriyama brought light to my darkened heart. Realizing how God had prepared my way even before I came, I thanked Him. As long as God was with me, this prison would not be as bad as hell. I recited chapter 54 of Isaiah. When I came to the last verse, I repeated it again.

> No weapon that is formed against thee shall prosper; and every tongue that shall rise against thee in judgment thou shalt condemn. This is the heritage of the servants of Jehovah, and their righteousness which is of me, saith Jehovah (Isaiah 54:17).

The food in the prison looked much better than the box lunch we were served at the detention house. The smell of the soup made me nauseated, but I closed my eyes and ate it with one sip. I had made up my mind to endure anything as a prisoner.

When I finished my first meal in the prison, I thanked God and, shutting my eyes, I pondered many things. Mother came into my thoughts. She never seemed to be upset. Although she was lonely, she was always clean, quiet, and pleasant, at peace within herself. Tears came easily to her, but they were tears of thanks, repentance, and of prayers for the unsaved. Because her heart was pure, she always worked diligently to make her surroundings clean, too, by washing, sweeping, and polishing the house. She was truly a living testimony of God's grace, strong spiritually and very dependable.

Once I teased her by telling her that her name is written in chapter 13 of the First Epistle to the Corinthians. "Love . . . bears all things, believes all things, hopes all things, endures all things" (vv. 4–7, NASB).

She was one of those persons who always lived for others. Once a week she filled a sack with aspirin, salve, candy, and tissue paper and visited the poor. I had never seen her eat warm rice. She would always cook a large amount of rice at one time.

"If I have plenty of cooked rice," she told me when I asked her about it, "I can give some to a beggar whenever he comes. In order to follow Jesus, I think we should always be prepared to give to others."

Mother was so different from the other members of my father's household. They only gave away that which they did not want to keep for themselves. They seemed to hate each other and only lived from day to day. They had no God, no holy day, no true joy or confidence. Wherever Mother was, it was like a chapel of heaven around her. As I remembered all of this about her, thankfulness to God for giving her to me arose in my heart.

"God," I prayed, "when I have accomplished this mission, award my mother the prize. I will be happy to die for You, anyway."

In a way, my prison cell was similar to my mother's marriage to my father. She was the daughter of a high government official in Seoul, and at the age of eight, she accepted Jesus through the efforts of a missionary. At that time there was neither a Korean church nor a Korean Bible. She had no Christian friends, but the missionary taught her these four principles to live by:

1. Jesus is the only Son of God and is the only Savior.
2. Jesus will never forsake His believers.
3. Jesus is able to take all the misfortunes of believers and turn them into good for the believers.
4. Jesus hears the prayers of His children.

About that time there was an upheaval in the imperial court, and most of the government officials were killed. My grandparents barely escaped with the help of three servants, hiding in a remote place in Kabsan where prisoners were banished. When she was twelve, the family left there to look for her husband to be, a youth who they thought was most suitable.

She experienced great mental strain with her many new relatives, enduring tense days as the wife of the firstborn. Because she had no sons, my father had many concubines. She left my father and went out to Pyongyang with me when I was still quite young.

Although I was given the best education possible, she knew that education could not solve the problems of life. The loving God, alone, was the key to all things.

Gradually Christ also became my King, and the words of the Bible became the promises to save me, just as had happened with my mother. Having been overwhelmed by God's infinite love and glowing with love for Jesus, I looked forward to being persecuted and tortured for His sake as a trial of my faith.

I had read the Bible several times and stored God's Word, will, and promises within my heart. I was prepared. I thought I would probably be able to give a good answer in this test. This was truly the trial I had been waiting for.

"Go to sleep!" a female jailer who had just come on duty ordered huskily. At the same time a distant sound of a trumpet was heard. The sound seemed to declare something very grave. Just then a soft voice came to me, as if whispering that the heavy iron gate of the prison was shut forever.

"O Lord," I prayed, "lend me Thy hand."

The extended, faraway sound of the trumpet sounded as if Satan were laughing and glaring proudly at me. I felt as though my chest had been pressed with a heavy stone, and my hands and legs were bound tightly.

I began to recite Bible verses, one after another. Gradually I regained calmness and strength. I found myself becoming light and full of Spirit, as if I had found light in the darkness. I kept reciting Scripture until I came to the book of Isaiah. "Fear thou not, for I am with thee; be not dismayed, for I am thy God; I will strengthen thee; yea, I will help thee; yea, I will uphold thee with the right hand of my righteousness. Behold, all they that were incensed against thee shall be put to shame and confounded" (Isaiah 41:10–11).

I felt as if a trumpet had been sounding forth loudly and strongly from my mouth and as though the sound had been ringing in every corner of the prison. Because of this trumpet of triumph, the other trumpet ordering us to sleep seemed to be fleeing farther and farther in search of a place to hide itself.

I began to think of Mother again. We used to get up at four in the morning and go to church together to pray. We forbade ourselves to talk until we finished our prayers at church, so we walked in silence until we came to a Japanese shrine along the road. My mother stopped suddenly and looked toward heaven. Then she stomped the ground and said, "Perish and disappear! In the name of Jesus Christ who has risen from the dead to live forever." She repeated those words three times. On the way from church, she would do the same thing.

"Mother," I said to her, "the Japanese now have all of Korea within their shrine, and their nation is among the strongest in all the world. *What do you think just one person can do?*"

"In God's sight," she said quietly, "one person with true

faith in Him is far more important than a thousand without faith. Abraham and Moses and David all stood alone. They were called and served God as individuals. I believe God is the same today."

The words of 2 Chronicles were surely true, I thought. "For the eyes of Jehovah run to and fro throughout the whole earth, to show himself strong in the behalf of them whose heart is perfect toward him" (16:9).

"I'm only an ignorant woman," Mother continued, "and only follow the will of God. I'll go against the idol and beseech that the will of God also shall be mine." Power was in her eyes, and her expression gave me an even stronger impression. The only strength within her was the desire to follow God to the end without wavering. I thought we could do something effectively with God's almighty power, Mother's faith and prayers, and the language I had acquired in school in Japan. Believing this, I would rise at four in the morning with Mother and go to church to pray.

Today the Japanese boasted of themselves as being the most outstanding people in the world. They proclaimed that their gods were to be worshiped by all people. I continued reciting verses of the Bible, while recalling those early morning walks to church.

"Devils, come out!" I cried. "I am a servant of God and am going to tell of the love of Jesus Christ and His saving power highly and widely throughout the world." In my excitement, I pounded on the floor with my fists.

As the night advanced, chinch bugs crawled out from the ceiling, walls, and floor. Seeing such a large host of insects crawling in my direction frightened me. They were as tiny as dust and as swift as though they had wings. Some of those that fell on me from the ceiling bit me savagely, but most only crawled over me.

Chinch bugs are creatures of the night, just as Satan's devils who live in a dark world of sin but would flee from the light of Jesus. If all of those ugly bugs had swarmed onto me and sucked my blood, within a few days I would not have had one drop of blood left. Strangely, however, only a few bit me. Seeing this made me realize that the devils would also flee from me. When dawn approached, the ugly insects were gone. When would morning also come to this land and make the powers of darkness disappear?

At three in the morning I woke up as usual. My prayer time was so regular that I would not need to see a clock. The time slipped by quickly while I was praying. Soon the trumpet sounded to waken us. It was getting light, and the new day came. The door to my cell opened noisily and I was ordered to run to the wash place and wash my face.

As I ran barefooted along the concrete corridor, I heard female prisoners talking to each other. I turned the faucet, washed my face quickly, and ran back at once.

Someone in cell two must not have been running fast enough to suit the angry jailer. She hit her on the head with her heavy ring of keys. On her way back, she was hit again and came back to her cell crying. I guessed that she was ill or that her legs were not functioning properly after being beaten.

After breakfast, which was exactly the same as supper, there was the morning inspection. A lunatic seemed to be confined to cell seven. She talked loudly in Korean.

"Inspect my cell, too!" she called out. "Bring me a man or I won't let you inspect. Hee, hee, hee!"

Neither the chief nor the jailer paid any attention to her. A hairpin was found in cell fifteen. That was enough to create a real fuss, as they questioned the inmates about it, trying to discover where it came from. Finally the noisy morning inspection was over and the two jailers who had been on duty were replaced and left. One of the new jailers stopped in front of my cell. She appeared to be frightened as she stood before me.

"Oh, you are Number 57," she said. "Isn't this a good number?"

I was pleasantly surprised by the tone of her voice. "What may I call you, ma'am?"

148

"They call me Madam or Master, but never mind about such a thing," she told me softly. "My name is Jue. I can never change my name the way the Japanese ordered us to. It has been used for hundreds of years in my family. I tell them to call me Miss Red, because Jue means red."

I was astonished. "In this time when those who do not have Japanese names are considered to have dangerous thoughts and are treated bitterly, how can you say such a thing? You are very fortunate."

She did not answer me. "I can't understand how your father, who is wealthy and pro-Japanese, let you come to such a place as this hell."

"I will probably be able to tell you the reason someday. But it was not my father but Someone who is far greater who told me to come here."

"That's God, isn't it, who is far greater than your father?"

"How did you know?"

"I'm a Christian."

"How wonderful!"

"Is it so wonderful to be a Christian?" she asked me dubiously, trying to read my face.

As I talked with her, I worshiped God within my heart, thanking Him for sending this Christian to be one of my jailers. Miss Jue had only been at the prison as a jailer for a month. God had sent her and Kuriyama to be in charge of me. Jailer Jue checked the cells only once and stayed near me for the remainder of her duty time, talking without reservation. It made me wonder if God had sent me here for a rest rather than to be imprisoned. She wanted to tell me about herself.

She told me about her unhappy marriage, and about leaving her husband and returning to her mother's home where she was also treated badly. Her mother wouldn't allow her to go to church, and she didn't fully understand God's love.

"I heard at church that the pastors and elders who were the closest to God were imprisoned," she said, "so finally I came here and took the test. I was employed in spite of the fact that

I did not do very well on the test. It's hard to look at the corruption. Everything is inconsistent here. I can hardly tolerate working at such a place, but since you have come I think I'll be able to endure."

The jailer who took her place was a grumpy middle-aged Japanese woman. She stopped at my cell and questioned me as she made her rounds. I watched her cautiously. I never knew what sort of violence she might commit against me. Actually, she might attack anyone without reason, like an ignorant and untrained dog, so I had to be extremely careful.

When Jue came back on duty, she told me everything she knew about the prison. Like Kuriyama, she also said that she hated the chief female jailer, and then she went on to tell me how repugnant the jailers were. Many wicked prisoners had power, and they humiliated her, Kuriyama, and others. While listening to her, I felt as though cold water had been dashed on my back. Her duty was over in an hour. I closed my eyes and prayed.

Since the wicked and convicted prisoners reported everything that took place in the cells to the most troublesome jailers, both Kuriyama and Jue had to be very careful. One girl was said to have reported anything that she heard. She was only sixteen but had four previous convictions and enjoyed causing trouble. After having been involved in several fights, she was now handcuffed and confined in her cell.

After inspection one morning, she informed the chief jailer that she had something to report. Returning from the chief jailer's room, she looked triumphant. As a result of that interview, Kuriyama was taken away, and from then on I realized that I was being watched. Jue also was taken from my sight, and the prison changed into a dark and dreadful place.

The jailers did not beat me, but seeing and hearing the other female prisoners being beaten made me tremble in fear. I decided to fast and pray for three days in order to receive God's special help. That three-day fast seemed harder than my previous ten-day fast. The prison coldness penetrated my bones, and I was shaking day and night. The prisoners in charge of the meals worried about me and encouraged me to eat. The jailer reported to her superior that I was not eating, so the prison doctor was called to examine me.

He took my temperature and checked my heart. "Her pulse is as weak as that of someone who is dying," he commented to no one in particular. "I'm amazed that she could live until now."

He directed his attention to me. "You have a fever, too," he said. Then, lowering his voice, he whispered, "Cheer up."

My fast came to an end the following day. The medicine and rice gruel were sent to me from the medical division. I sipped the liquid medicine, which was in a large bottle. It was not medicine at all but was candy melted in water. It tasted so delicious that I finished the entire bottle. My frozen, shrunken body felt so light that I felt as if I could fly. Adding to my joy, warm sunshine was coming in from the window high above. The agony of the three-day fast was over. Now, what happiness! I thanked my heavenly Father again and again.

On the other hand, the cold wind blowing in from the holes in the floor was as sharp as a sword. They seemed to be mocking me, and when evening came I had to fight the savage cold even more. Would there be a miracle or would each cell of my body freeze to death? Death itself was not dreadful, but the agony that would precede it haunted me.

Morning came at last, and it seemed like a miracle to me that I had not died. It was snowing now, each flake an enemy soldier, lying with that infinite army to attack me with an onslaught of unrelenting cold.

I remembered the prayer that the prophet Elijah had cried out when he had fled to the wilderness in fear of Queen Jezebel: "It is enough; now, O Jehovah, take away my life" (1 Kings 19:4).

The power that imperial Japan was now exercising was greater than that of Queen Jezebel. Even nature seemed to be on the side of the Japanese. I coughed more violently because I knew that blood would follow a heavy period of coughing. My lungs would dry up, I reasoned, if I coughed hard enough. But my heart darkened as I realized that this slow death would be the same as committing suicide.

I looked out the window and saw a bird trembling on a bare bough that had long ago withered. I was just like that bird. Suddenly I shook my head to the right and left vigorously. That courageous bird was playing in a swirling snowstorm, ignoring her enemies. I had to be such a bird. If she only perched on that withered bough with her head stuck beneath her wing and feared the wind, snow, heaven, earth, and everything else that might challenge her, she would only freeze and die when night came. I cried out.

> Fly, fly, servant of God,
> Fly high up in the sky with your utmost strength,
> Without ceasing, without fear, keep on flying.

My faith was so weak. I wanted to sob out my sadness and vexation. Although Jesus' holy power was infinite and His promises true, why wasn't I able to walk bravely and cheerfully, loving and trusting Him? I wanted to cry, but if I did the jailers would think Christians were miserable. Instead, I sang hymns loudly, one after another, risking the danger of being rebuked for it.

"Awake, O north wind," I sang from the Song of Solomon, "and come, wind of the south; make my garden breathe out fragrance, let its spices be wafted abroad" (4:16 NASB).

I felt my heart widen and heighten like a clear, blue sky. Suddenly the door to my cell was opened and the jailer threw in a large package. There was a complete set of clothing, consisting of a silk coat, underwear, and socks. The new clothes were quilted with cotton for warmth. When I took off my dirty prison uniform and dressed in the new clothes, I felt that all my world had changed. I spread out the thick Russian blanket and sat on it. My heart full of thankfulness, I knelt down and worshiped God.

I was no longer trembling. My anxiety turned to joy, and I continued singing thanks to God as the songs arose in my heart.

The cold of the winter increased in intensity, and even with good, warm clothes it kept me from sleeping. The number of prisoners in the women's ward had been increased over the weeks until all the cells were filled. Several were moved into my cell, which made it a little warmer than when I was alone.

The food made us feel even more hungry after we had eaten it. All we thought about or talked about was food. I wanted sweets more than anything else.

When the meal was served, my portion seemed less than that of the others, yet everyone complained that my portion was more than theirs. I exchanged my food for theirs only to prove that each serving was the same.

When bedtime came it was impossible for us to sleep, we were so hungry. This type of hunger was quite different from that of fasting. There was a desperation in it.

26

ON TRIAL

One morning in January, the coldest month of the year, two male jailers and a female guard took me to the male ward and on to the office. Only then did I realize that I was to be brought before the court. I raised my eyes and looked to the sky. The day was bitterly cold. The sky, the clouds, and even the air appeared to be frozen, but somehow that gray, forbidding universe seemed warm and friendly to me.

Throwing me a pair of straw sandals, the jailer commanded me to put them on. Then he placed a braided straw hat on my head. It was so big that it completely hid my head and my face as it reached to my shoulders. There were two tiny holes through which I could see outside. After handcuffing me, the jailer bound me with a heavy rope.

I sang triumphantly in my heart. A worthless person such as I was going to testify of the Lord's precious Gospel! As I looked through the two holes, the back door opened and other believers were brought in.

Reverend Chae was the first! I bent from my waist deeply,

bowing many times to him, but he did not recognize me because of the hat. Impetuously I raised the hat with my handcuffed hands.

"Oh!" he cried out, greeting me by bowing in return.

Although he looked even more haggard than before, probably because of starvation, his face was radiant. Reverend Joo followed him like a lamb following its shepherd. Many other Christian leaders were in the room that day. I recognized many but could not see them all. These noble servants of God were roped together and taken to the court.

These noble servants of God were forced to put on Japanese sandals and long braided straw hats. They were also handcuffed and bound in a row with a long, heavy rope. I was told to follow in the middle. The large main gate was swung open by two guards to allow us to leave the prison. I raised my eyes. The sun was hidden behind the clouds. Softly I prayed.

"Lord, all of the human race is rebelling against You. But we, though such a small number, are bound because we don't want to rebel. We're sorry to be so few, but please be with us. We know nothing about our future. Rule everything until our lives shall come to an end and until the moment when we shall worship You face-to-face."

The street was completely frozen, and the snow had been packed so hard that it was as smooth and as slippery as glass. The onlookers were curious and interested in the fact that I was a woman. I must have been an evil woman, they said aloud. Perhaps I had even killed someone. They looked on me with contempt, clacking their tongues. I recalled Jesus carrying His cross and walking toward the hill of Golgotha. The crowd that had been fed with the bread and fish and had been healed of their illnesses through the compassion of Christ had hurried to hang Him on the cross. I felt as though I could see His face that day as He stumbled along under the weight of the cross.

That was a horrible day. Reverend Chae was whipped because he could not walk fast enough and fell behind. A young unconvicted prisoner was placed at the head of the line. When the jailer yelled, the young prisoner ran, causing a number of believers, including Reverend Chae to fall. Blood soaked the white hair of that battered old saint, staining his white garments and the icy street.

"Hurry, hurry, Lord!" I cried out in agony. "Send Your heavenly camera and take pictures of this atrocity. See how terrible this persecution is! And how faithful the believers are!"

The cruel treatment, far from breaking our spirit, strengthened us.

When we reached the court, all the families of the imprisoned Christians were there, including Mother. She looked full of confidence. I wondered how they had heard that the trial was about to be held. The only explanation I could find was that the Korean jailers had secretly informed our families and other believers. They welcomed us by loudly singing one of Martin Luther's hymns, "God Is My Refuge and Strength."

One jailer poured water on the people who were singing. Since the weather was extremely cold, the water froze immediately, but they continued to sing even more loudly than before. The guards quickly and forcefully chased us into the confinement room.

They removed the rope and the braided hats, but the handcuffs remained, colder than ice and so heavy that I soon started to shake uncontrollably. My breathing began to sound like the wheezing of an old car, and the pain almost made me senseless.

The jail inspector opened the door of the dark cell I was in. "She won't run away," he said. "Take them off."

The youthful jailer removed the handcuffs.

When I was taken into court, the judge was already in his place. The attorney was beside him and two secretaries faced each other, sitting at a table directly below the judge. "With what words and attitudes and threats were they going to convict the innocent?" I asked myself. I felt so amused that I was about to burst into laughter.

The sinners were going to judge the just. In pomp, they were scorning the believers and planning to slaughter the men of God. The time was coming when they would see who we were, whether they willed it or not. The living God would rebuke them and reveal their awful acts. We would not fear any man. Then I would declare plainly the perfect and abiding law of the Almighty. I had been living for this purpose. My love for my Savior was finally going to be proved.

"Keep watching me, Jesus," I prayed. "I want to testify clearly today at this moment that You, Lord, are the only living God."

Outside, our families and the other believers were still singing loudly. The jailers were throwing water at them and threatening to beat them, but they sang even louder than before, so loudly, in fact, that it was difficult to hear the judge's voice. Seeing that he was perplexed, I asked if I could go out and stop their singing.

He gave me permission and I dashed out, with the two secretaries, the jailer, and the jail inspector a few steps behind me. The crowd was even bigger than before, and when they saw me they sang even louder, greeting me by raising both their hands. I also raised my hands high and waved to stop their singing.

"Now I must testify of the true God," I told them, "but the judge cannot hear me because of your singing. Would you please pray for me instead of singing?"

I watched Mother who was standing in the front.

"The Lord is with you," she said when I finished. "Don't be afraid. Be courageous."

The great crowd bowed their heads and chorused, "Amen."

They were praying when I went back into the courtroom.

"What leadership!" one of the secretaries whispered. "She can do anything."

I waited in anticipation to hear what the judge would say. "You seem to have great leadership ability," he said to me. "Why don't you try to serve your nation with your gift?"

I did not answer him.

"According to your protocol, you acted against the law of imperial Japan and are a very dangerous and unpardonable criminal. Is that right?"

"All that is written in the protocol is true."

I was calm and pleasant and even felt amused. I felt that the Lord on His throne, along with His host of angels and martyrs, was listening to my testimony.

"You have received the best possible education," the judge continued. "You are intelligent and have been brought up in a wealthy family, a situation other women would envy. With your leadership ability and initiative, you should be able to lead people in whatever way you wish. For what purpose have you been allured to ruin yourself, disorder society, and bring great loss to the nation?"

"Mr. Judge," I said, "would you listen to me? What would you do if you saw someone who was drinking sewage water without knowing how filthy it was, and if he was telling others to drink it as well? I'm sure you would tell him not to drink it. Perhaps, if telling him would bring disgrace to you, you might keep silent. But I cannot. Whatever danger or disgrace might be brought upon me, I must run up to the person and tell him not to drink the water. Jesus Christ, the Son of God in whom I have faith with all my might, died for such a purpose and has taught me to live accordingly. Therefore, though I might be killed or imprisoned for it, I must testify of the truth and save the person who is drinking the sewage water."

"Who do you mean is drinking the sewage water?" he demanded.

"Imperial Japan! The Japanese police force, that is beating and killing the saints of God, is drinking the sewage water. For this reason I went to Tokyo and warned the important officials in the Japanese Diet. Those saints whom the Japanese government officials have been torturing didn't receive the Japanese education I did. Because of their inability to speak, they are murdered one after another by the most cruel and merciless torture.

"Let me tell you how blind and crazy the Japanese government officials are. They trust the most malicious two-faced persons, promote them, honor them, and make them prosper in order to destroy the Christian Church and bring a curse upon the nation. Who would God help? Is there any nation remaining today that has not rebelled against Almighty God and persecuted Christians? History speaks the truth. Today Japan is obviously rebelling against the true God. There are many famous Christian leaders in Japan to choose from, but God has called me, a Korean, to warn the Japanese government."

Suddenly feeling overwhelmed, I was unable to continue. Although I had promised myself that I would not lose my temper or cry, the tears flowed spontaneously. I sensed that God, with His host of angels, was filling the room and was watching over me. Otherwise, why would this judge and the prosecutor have listened to what I had said? It was truly miraculous. There was a brief discussion between the judge and one of the prosecutors. Then I was taken out, with the jailer and jail inspector following me.

"It was totally amazing," the secretary said. "How could you explain such a thing?"

"The judge was like a prisoner," the jail inspector observed, "and Number 57 was like a chief judge."

I didn't know whether the judge was impressed or struck silent by my impudence. My heart was cheerful, as though I had just finished a final exam and knew that I had done well. I thanked God.

"You must have closed their mouths tightly so I could speak," I prayed. "I know it well. Lord, I long to die for You, because I love You more than anything or anyone else in all the world."

I recalled the story of Reverend Kil. Now I could understand his prayer. "Heavenly Father," he prayed while he was praying through the night, "this is enough. Do not pour any more blessings upon me, for I am content."

The other Christians were called one by one, and each returned quickly. They were all handcuffed, covered with the long straw hats, and bound in a row in order to be sent back to the prison. The crowd that had been waiting outside throughout the trials started to sing "All Hail the Power of Jesus' Name" thunderously as we came out.

As I looked at the other prisoners getting out of the bus that had transported us from the place of the trials to the prison, my heart broke. Eventually they would starve and die in prison. In the end the survivors would all be killed at once.

Oh, what noble martyrs they were! They would surely remember the gates of this prison when they would go through the gate of heaven. They would tell Jesus it was because of His love and not because of their own powers that they had not denied their faith.

How happy and joyous they would all be then! There would be so much to tell Jesus that we would continue talking with Him forever. While listening to their stories, I would remember and rejoice over how desperate I had been to love the Lord Jesus Christ with all my might. How I would thank God for this suffering!

Oh, is this really me? I thought. *It's unbelievable!*

27

MEMORIES

The sulky summer had come. Flies swarmed by the thousands around the smelly toilet bowl in the cell. Mosquitoes swarmed through the open windows to attack us, and at night the chinch bugs joined them. Like the mosquitoes, they carried diseases, and many in the ward were sick because of them. However, the bugs seemed to have no interest in me. I was seldom bit and never became sick because of them.

A more severe attack came upon us by starvation. It was a common fact that all the prisoners would rather have eaten until they were full than to have been spared from the diseases carried by the insects. I was hungry not only for food, but for color. The monotonous red brick of the prisoner's clothes made my eyes tired. It was not relieved by the gray uniforms of the jailers and unconvicted prisoners.

To help my eyes a little I would look up at the blue sky and white clouds through the tiny window high on the wall. That helped, but I longed to see those wild chrysanthemums that add such sweet, refreshing beauty to the wide autumn fields. I wished to see the multicolored rose moss which bloomed in springtime and grew around the stepping-stones of the garden and by the fence. I also wanted to see the zinnias that bloomed in the rain, or those slender and tall cosmos with their soft, green leaves. How I wanted to see the vivid shades of green that hid the mountains in early spring, the grass on the slopes, and the trees and woods!

I also was starved for the beauty of music, for my favorite records of piano, violin, and cello, and the intriguing melody of human voices. If only I could sing out so beautifully to praise my Lord! These were pains and hunger that few of the other prisoners would understand.

Ever since I was a child I had sung constantly on my way to and from church and school. I even liked to hear people weep because it sounded musical. It may sound strange, but I enjoyed going to the public cemetery on the Festival Day of the Dead, August 15, and on the day in February set aside to visit the graves of the dead. I would climb a pine tree and look down at the crowd of people who came to place food by the graves of their loved ones. Then the men would kneel and worship their dead families while the women would cry out in unison, *"Aigo, aigo."*

I could not understand why, but the women in my household were greatly comforted in going to the cemetery in the mountain and crying there. It was particularly difficult for me to understand how they could be so grief-stricken at the grave of my grandmother when she had been so strict and harsh before her death that none of them liked her.

Once on our way home from the cemetery I asked one of my nurses about it. "Why do they now cry so sadly in front of her grave?"

"I'm sure they are not crying in fond remembrance of her," she said. "I think they cry out because of the hardship of this world. There is no place other than the cemetery in front of a grave where they can cry over the hardship of life."

I could never forget this conversation. They would save up

all their hardship and sadness of the entire year, waiting for the day of visiting the cemetery. I wondered if the world was actually so hard and sad.

But Mother always had been different from the others. I had never seen her crying, nor had she ever shown tears in front of other people. She also never laughed aloud that I was aware of. On the other hand, she didn't seem to know how to get angry. At the time of my grandmother's death, the relatives all gathered before her coffin and wept aloud for her, each in his mourning clothes. Everyone was crying except my mother, who had never cried aloud in her life.

One of my aunts poked her in the side. "Cry, Sister," she whispered. "Cry loudly or they might criticize you."

My mother was frightened by the warning. With all her effort she made a noise that didn't come out like she had intended it to. "Eheh-eh-eh!"

It was such a funny sound that my aunt could not contain herself but burst out laughing, "Oh, my goodness!" The laughter spread to another aunt and then to another. It became contagious, spreading from one to another until finally it reached the attention of my father's sisters.

"My goodness! Are you all so happy that our mother has died?" they demanded haughtily.

The men looked around, and it was obvious that they, themselves, were laughing instead of crying. My father's sisters became even more furious and stood up. My other aunts all stopped crying, but my mother was still faithfully working at it. Her voice was so funny that the men's faces became red, and they had to look down to keep from laughing again. At last my father's sisters recognized my mother's voice. Knowing that she had never been able to cry or laugh aloud, they realized that they could do nothing about it and their tempers calmed.

However, a strange rumor spread in the little town of Bak Chon. The story said that all the in-laws and sons had burst out in joy instead of wailing because that wealthy grandmother at the Ahns had been so hard and strict while she was alive. But since the cause of the rumor had been my mother's actions, the matter did not get worse because of the rumors. My mother was greatly respected and trusted and loved in her household.

Neither could Mother sing hymns. Her singing consisted of reading the words with the rhythm of the songs. She always had a peaceful smile, and occasionally I detected tears in her eyes, for the joy in the Lord was so great within her.

With nothing to do, the days for us in prison were long. I recalled my old memories more and more, and the thoughts of food never left my mind. My father's household was proud of their big celebration on New Year's Day and other festivals. Some of the women boiled rice for cakes, some pounded the rice, others fried it. There were sweets made from green beans, chestnuts, persimmons, and pine seeds, along with broiled and fried beef, pork, and chicken. All kinds of gay voices and scents spread throughout the house.

Such a day would not return to me again.

As a believer, I felt I should be thinking of things more noble and holy, but what a shameful and miserable reality! The thought that I might die of hunger and not be able to join the martyrs made me gloomy. Didn't I even have a little of a saintly nature, or did I only have a beggar's stomach?

As I thought of the past, I remembered how I used to enjoy seeing a funeral procession. The chief mourner in coarse linen clothes and the other men in the household in the same clothes made two rows, walking in front of the casket. They held sticks in their hands and chorused, *"Aigo, aigo,"* to express their sorrow. Behind the casket were the women, who were dressed in the same way.

Men hired especially for this occasion walked forward and backward, carrying the casket on their shoulders. On top of the casket was a professional man speaking for the dead and chanting sadly, as if the dead person himself had been speaking.

"How many years have passed since I was born in this town?" he would say mournfully. "Have I not lived over fifty years from childhood to adolescence, from middle age to this day, laughing at one time and crying at another time?"

In answer, the mourners would cry in unison, *"Aigo, aigo."*

"This is my eternal farewell to you all, for I am unable to return to this world again. Oh, my beloved wife, my dear children, and my dear townsmen, shed tears at this eternal farewell and save me. Though I have now become invisible, how can I ever forget this town, this road, and this house, wherever I may roam?"

"Aigo, aigo."

"With many unforgettable memories in my heart, I shall now be gone forever."

"Aigo, aigo."

"Knowing that I would have to go to the other world, how much more had I struggled to live longer in this town."

"Aigo, aigo."

The emotionally weak women would follow, crying out in mourning. Some of the onlookers also cried. I would often cry in sympathy.

The funeral of a Christian, however, was quite different. The same type of mourning clothes would be worn, but the believers would gather at the church, and a pastor would officiate. All who were present would sing in mourning, but also with hope.

The pastor explained the fullness of peace in heaven and how the Lord had prepared to receive us at the time of our death. The family of the deceased and friends were in tears, but everything was far different from the sadness of the unbelievers.

Although the promises of Jesus gave me strength and hope while in prison, hunger continually taunted me. The book of Job described me well. Living was a burden, and everything seemed too heavy for me to bear. When would death call me? When would I be relieved from hunger? When could I quit fighting this cold? Suddenly I envisioned hell. The chief jailer, the wicked jailers, and the most vile of the prisoners were probably not afraid of hell. All of them seemed to like this detestable prison and acted as though they wanted to live here forever. They might, therefore, be the ones suitable for hell. They didn't know God and had nothing to depend upon.

My thoughts turned to the days when I was going to college in Kyoto. My mother's youngest brother was studying at Kyoto Imperial University and had a very close college friend born in Tokyo, the member of a fine family. He was tall and handsome, and his eyes were so beautiful I could think of little else when he was around. When he came to the home where I was living, my heart would become restless and I couldn't concentrate on anything. And when he didn't come for some time, I would long to see him. He was one of the few college students who went to church regularly, and he seemed particularly close to the pastor and his wife.

One day when my uncle and his friend and I went to a mountain river to swim, I wanted to dive. But I became nervous and fell from a fifty-foot cliff, slamming into the water so hard that it knocked the breath from my lungs. The young man moved faster than my uncle, diving in and rescuing me. While being held in his arms, I felt like fainting.

After that incident he visited frequently with my uncle, but he would never come into my room unless my uncle was with him. One day my uncle asked him about it.

"She is a man-hater," he replied. "I'm afraid that she'll hate me." "She owes you her life," my uncle told him. "She can never hate you."

Later my uncle told me that his friend was in love with me. When my uncle saw how nervous I was, he grinned and looked happy.

"To tell you the truth, I want to marry my professor's daughter," he said, "but my mother is opposing it so stubbornly that I don't know what I should do. You and I will probably end up committing suicide together."

"Oh, no, Uncle!" I cried. "You'll fall into hell!"

"I can't help it. We are, in fact, married already, even though we didn't have an official wedding."

I knew how strongly my grandmother and mother had opposed his marrying a Japanese girl.

"Would you convince them so that you can marry my friend and I can marry my professor's daughter?" he asked.

Before I left to go back to Korea to teach school, my uncle's friend asked me to request the permission from my mother and return to Japan. Upon returning home, I first asked Grandmother and Mother to allow my uncle to marry the Japanese girl he loved. Both were so strongly opposed to it that I knew there was no use in bringing my own request to them. I had promised my friend that I would not write unless I could obtain permission to marry him, so I was unable to write even one letter to him.

During the coming months, my sister told me of three candidates to be my spouse and explained their backgrounds in detail. My mother rejected all of them. To her, it was almost a sin to force one as weak as I was into marriage.

I felt discouraged when I heard my mother speak as she did. Letters were arriving from my uncle and his friend almost every day. Mother could not read the letters in Japanese, but my sister could, so the secret had to come out. I told Mother everything and asked if both my uncle and I could marry our Japanese friends.

"To marry a Japanese," she said gently, "means to surrender to the idols that the Japanese worship. The Japanese themselves might be Christians, but as long as Japan and the Japanese people are controlled by idols, I don't believe it would be a good marriage."

I decided to ask for God's help. It was hard for me, but there was no way but to refrain from writing to my friend so that he would give up. More candidates were introduced to me to be my spouse, but Mother refused every one of them. I felt loneliness deep in my heart and tried to overcome it, but I still felt unsatisfied.

When shrine worship was becoming more strict and enforced, several pastors who regretted my detainment visited me and gave me their heartfelt counsel.

"Remember that you are only a simple believer," they said. "You're neither a pastor nor an evangelist. Our God is not going to blame you so severely if you worship the Japanese shrine. Moreover, you're not a man but still just a young, unmarried woman. Our God would not force unreasonable things on anybody."

They believed that because the Japanese had been forcing us to worship, God would look over us if we worshiped the shrine. This might have been true, but in my own heart, because of my love for God I could not violate His law and ask Him to overlook it. I felt His love more deeply than ever. I decided to stand firm on His love.

Seeing me with tears of thankfulness, one of the prisoners wept for me. "I feel sorry for you because such a respectable young lady as you must suffer from hunger. I don't blame you for crying."

Another prisoner sitting beside her said, "Be quiet if you don't understand. She is not crying like you because she wants to eat. She is talking with God in her heart, and she is crying for joy."

"Yes, yes," another prisoner said.

In hearing their conversation, I paid attention to them as though I had been awakened from a dream. They would talk about their husbands, their children, and about food, and often they would cry. But when somebody cried, the others openly showed their annoyance. I was overwhelmed with gratitude that these same prisoners were so generous toward me.

Even those prisoners who were full of anxiety knew my heart. How much more would God know my heart and embrace me with His warm compassion. My mother had not given me a square foot of land or a lot of money, but she had led me to the greatest treasure of heaven. For her love, I was endlessly thanking the Lord.

Christmas had come in the prison. It arrived amid the pathetic starvation and severe coldness and the heartbreaking torture by the most vulgar jailers. Christmas was indeed a joyous occasion. How I had sung praises to God on other Christmases and rejoiced with holiness pouring into my heart. But now I was being touched by a truth that I never before had known. God had truly sent His only Son into this dark and filthy world. He humbled Himself to be born as a man. He experienced poverty, weariness, sorrow, pain, and great persecution. He was hated and rejected, hit and spat upon, and was hung on the cross to die! And His death was for the purpose of saving such a sinful and worthless person as myself.

The more I thought of my Savior's sacrifice, the more pained I became. Wasn't the history of mankind passing by calmly as if ignorant of the sacred reality of the death of Christ? Men, what an unpardonable sin and evil ye dared commit!

"O Lord Jesus pardon us! Wilt thou still forgive and await for them to return to Thee?"

When I cried out these words, my body trembled strangely as if I were suddenly touched by electricity. My heart melted as tears flooded my eyes. My heart, my blood, my flesh, my nerves, and my bones were all crying. Had I been free I would have gone deep into the mountains, as my mother would always do, to cry until the grass would wither and the soil would be soaked. Why did the Lord love such a weakling and sinful child as myself so much?

Breathing heavily I looked up from my dark suffering to the Lord of the resurrection. He looked gloriously brilliant. Different from the ray of the sun that shone brightly, His radiance made no shadow, but it spread light throughout the world and softly veiled everything. This light was the light of salvation for every man, having come from the throne of Jehovah, going through the tomb in which Jesus had once been buried.

As this light came into my weeping heart, wouldn't I have

to follow the footsteps of Jesus more and more earnestly? I would be humiliated, hated, insulted, and maybe tortured and starved to death. Let me be prepared to be buried in agony!

What was the life of man? Now, sing with my greatest voice to praise the love of God!

28

THE
MANIAC

It was an extremely cold night. Through the crevice in the floor, a strong wind was blowing, a wind so cold that it felt like a thousand steel arrows piercing through me. The trumpet for retiring had blown, but it was impossible for me to sleep. Shivering, we all huddled together for warmth. Then we heard an eerie, moaning sound, like that of cows bellowing. It came from a nearby cell.

"What is that sound?" I asked a woman jailer who had stopped near our cell.

"That's the Chinese convict on the death roll. She's insane."

"Is she young?"

"She's only twenty years old. Her clothes are always soiled, and she kept pounding on her door until we tied her hands behind her. Now she curses that way. She deserves to be punished."

My heart went out to the poor woman. On such a cold night she was alone with her hands tied behind her back. In her soiled prison clothes I could imagine how she must feel. Her voice was rising and wavering in the cold. I strained to hear her as she mumbled the same words over and over. Even if she were insane, she would feel the cold.

I thought of Jesus. He healed and saved the sinners and the sick. If He were here, whom would He have visited first? Me? He would have passed by my cell to visit and help the insane woman. She was the one who needed Him the most.

"She killed her husband," the jailer went on. "Hacked his body into pieces and threw them into the river. She is a real devil; she isn't even human."

I pitied her and wanted to help her, but I tried to find an excuse for myself. After all, I was only a prisoner myself and she was a Manchurian. So even if I could get to help her, I couldn't talk to her. But her cursing seemed to be directed straight at me. Then I heard a voice from my heart! "Am I not a Christian who follows Jesus? Isn't it right to do what Jesus did? He would not leave her like this. Would He say it was all right if I did not help her?"

I was unable to sleep the rest of the night because of the hunger and cold, but mostly because I was thinking about the poor, frightened girl. She was lying on the floor, her hands behind her. She had to crawl like a dog to eat the scraps off the floor. During the day, she was fairly quiet, but as night approached her terrible cursing began once more.

"Let's pray that we can bring her to our cell," I told the women in my cell. They seemed surprised, but I didn't mind.

On the fourth day I called the jailer and asked if she would bring her to our cell. "I want to help her before she is hanged," I explained.

"She's crazy. She bites everybody."

"I know, but would you move her into our cell?"

The jailer refused. As soon as she left for the day, I tried to explain to the new jailer, but it was useless. She would not listen to me either.

Finally, I asked another jailer. She went to the chief jailer about it. "She wants to know why you want that," she asked me.

"The poor woman is an alien," I said. "And she is about to

172

be sentenced to death in a foreign country where the language and customs are different from hers. I want to talk to her, if I can, and be with her before she dies."

The chief jailer relayed the request to the prison commander, who gave his permission. In the late afternoon a male jailer came and dragged and pushed her into my cell.

The stench from her clothing was so overpowering that the other prisoners clustered in the far corner, holding their noses. Her hair was long and disheveled, and her eyes were sunken and reddened. She hadn't washed for a long time and she looked as though she wanted to bite everyone.

I held her from the back. As I suspected, she struggled desperately to free herself, trying as hard as she could to bite my hands. We both fell to the floor, but I didn't let her go. The more she tried to pull away from me, the more tightly I held her. I was desperate and so was she. We struggled all over the cell. The prisoners backed away from us, wondering what would happen next.

Finally we both were so exhausted that we fell flat on the floor. Her breathing was heavy and her eyes were glossy. She struggled no longer but glared fiercely at me. Finally she fell asleep. Her bare feet were covered with her excrement, but I didn't want to wake her up due to the cold. I took her feet into my bosom and held them against my chest to keep them warm.

When midnight came, I woke with a start and found that her snoring was disturbing everyone. It was so noisy that the other prisoners complained and were unable to sleep. Morning came, but she continued sleeping. She slept through the meal. I continued to hold her legs and feet against my body to warm them. As her cold prison clothing was being warmed, the stench increased. The other prisoners found it difficult to bear and were complaining loudly about it, but the poor girl slept through it all. For three days she snored on.

When her snoring became weaker, she finally woke up. Discovering that her legs were in my bosom, she pulled them out angrily. Because she had slept so much, her eyes were swollen.

I called the jailer and asked if she could have clean clothes. The guards brought her the fresh clothes, and when the jailer unlocked her handcuffs she fainted.

"You are with this dirty beast, and you can still eat your meal?" one of the guards asked me.

"I didn't know it was this hard to be a Christian," one prisoner said.

I massaged the girl's body and gradually she regained consciousness. She was still glaring savagely at me and cursing. I helped her to eat the meal which had been stored for her for three days. She quickly ate up all the frozen food.

When we had struggled she sweated so much that her eyes, which had been crusty with mucus, were now cleansed. Her face, which had been like dirty leather, became human again. Still, she glared and cursed at me. But I could not give her up. While carefully paying attention to her, I prayed to God for guidance.

Jesus Himself was participating in this battle, I realized. Surely my gratitude was beyond words. By nature, I would have tried to ignore the girl with all my might, but in reality exactly the opposite was happening. Here I was, holding a woman who was unspeakably dirty. Only Jesus' mercy could cause me to do it.

Jesus knew I was selfish, weak, deceitful, and sinful. But He treated me as valuable and important. How could I avoid her simply because she was so dirty in my eyes? To Him, we were the same.

Because of her cold, painful hunger, she needed exercise and rest, so the Lord let me hold her as she struggled, sweated, and then slept for three days. What was the Lord's plan now?

The convicted murderer glared stubbornly at me and wouldn't stop cursing. About this time a newcomer was brought to our cell. She had been engaged in black marketing between Korea and Manchuria and could speak the convicted killer's language.

"That dirty Chinese!" she exploded. "'I'm going to kill her!" She reprimanded the girl in Manchurian and tried to seize her hair. I stopped the trouble between the two and had the black marketeer sit in the rear so she would not approach the woman they said was insane. I learned one phrase of Manchurian, "That's right."

When the cursing continued, I nodded and gently said in Manchurian, "That's right." She would stop, then, for a time. The black marketeer scolded her and seemed to explain something to her. Her expression, as she looked at me, changed slightly.

Presently, she went to sleep again, and I sheltered her legs on my heart. While she was sleeping I learned a few more words in Manchurian so I could say, "I like you" and "I love you." I discovered that it was an easy language to learn.

When her meal came, she glared at us fiercely and tried to eat the meal of one of the other prisoners. I gave her mine. She ate my lunch and supper, yet she hated me.

In her own language I told her that I loved her. Baffled, she looked at me. Then contempt drove the confusion away and she turned from me. As I spoke to her, an unexpected miracle was happening in my heart. "I truly like you," I said, love for her filling my heart. In my intense love for her, tears streamed from my eyes.

On the following day I gave her my three meals. I cherished this experience in my heart with thanksgiving and deep joy. I was happy and excited from accomplishing a responsibility given to me by God.

I wanted to eat my breakfast, but since I had decided to give her my food for three days I let her eat mine. She sipped the soup and her eyes responded. I wanted to say "I love you," but I couldn't because my voice had become hoarse. I was crying. She sat quietly, her eyes downcast. It seemed that she understood my feelings. When the jailer called the roll, she said, "Number 92 has changed."

I appealed to the chief jailer to unlock her handcuffs. When that was done, I massaged her body, crying as I did so. My tears were in gratitude to God and praise for the love of Jesus. My heart was as clear as a mountain stream.

I combed her tangled hair. Gradually she became prettier, and her voice made a pleasant impression on me. I simply watched her. "Your voice is truly pretty," I said, "and your eyes are pretty, too." I saw to it that none of the other prisoners insulted her.

Number 92 responded to the roll call like most of us, saluting the chief jailer.

"Is this the insane woman?" the jailer asked. "She really has changed."

I interpreted that for Number 92. Watching her convinced me of the love of Jesus who gave us the new birth in Christ. She was always aware of my presence, and the love of the Lord was upon her.

"Why do you like a person like me?" she asked.

I was so happy I wanted to dance for joy.

"Because we are in the same situation," I said.

"Did you kill your husband, too?" she asked.

I did not answer her question but repeated my answer. She felt relieved to know that the other prisoners were no different from her.

She looked relaxed now, but she did not seem to be able to laugh or smile. How could it be possible to make this death-roll convict laugh, except through Jesus Christ? One day as I was trying to tell a joke, I spoke Manchurian at random. It was funny Manchurian since I had mispronounced it. She found it to be very funny, I knew, but she did not laugh.

"Have you ever laughed?" I demanded irritably. She confessed that she hadn't.

"Have you ever cried?"

Again she shook her head.

What a miserable life she had led. She was like a rough desert that was completely parched. That night a full moon shined gently through the small window. Everyone was sighing and homesick, unable to sleep because of the cold and the hunger. Suddenly Number 92 cried out, "My baby! My darling boy, where are you?" Her face was streaked with tears. Sobbing out her anguish, she fell to the floor.

"Crying helps!" I said to her. I was also crying. "Cry hard."

"Just before I was arrested," she said, "I gave birth to a baby boy. Then the policemen arrived and took me to the station. They started to torture me and I couldn't give my baby any milk, so the detectives took him from me. Do you suppose he died?"

I could not answer her question.

The Manchurian woman who had never cried before in her entire life was now crying for the baby of her womb. I waited until she stopped.

"Do you hear a voice calling you from a distance?"

"No."

"Listen carefully," I said. "Somebody is calling you."

"Nobody calls for me."

"Your Creator is calling you."

She could not understand that.

"He is calling for you constantly. He is just like you. You can't forget about your child, because he's yours. He can't forget about you because you belong to Him."

"Oh, you are a missionary. Jesus Christ," she said. "Christmas, missionary, Bible," she murmured, as if to recollect something.

"Where did you learn those words?" I asked her.

"When I was a child a yellow-haired Westerner came to our village, gathered us children, and took us to a place called church. There I learned a song, 'Jesus loves me, this I know, for the Bible tells me so.'

"But my parents wanted me to work, so they didn't let me go to the church. Once I went without their consent and was beaten for it.

"When I was ten I was sold to an old man as his mistress

and was taken to a place where there was no church." In her anger and regret she bit her lips and was silent for a time. "My husband treated me better than my parents did, but I hated him. I escaped many times, but I had no place to go so I went back to him. Then I took revenge on my father and finally on my husband. Now I have great regret and pain because of what I have done. Is it wrong to take revenge, Miss Ahn?"

"Do you worry about it?"

"Ah," she mumbled, "what can I do now?"

"Jesus is very kind. He welcomes everyone to save them from troubles, sin, and death."

"But I did a dreadful thing. When I killed my husband, I cut up his body." She was trembling now, jerking with uncontrollable spastic movements, and her eyes were wide and staring. "Now I hate myself. I hate myself more than I hated my parents and my husband.

"Did my husband go to hell?"

"Perhaps."

"I'm sure he did." She was in such extreme agony that she bit her lips, twisted and pulled at her hair, and pounded her body with her fists. The night for her was long and cold and miserable.

When morning came, I looked at her. Her face was lovely and serene. Her long dark hair hung down her back, and her features were well composed. To my surprise, she was also sensitive and courteous, even though her education and family circumstances were limited and even tragic.

At the prison every morning a small piece of toilet paper was allotted each prisoner. But because of the small amount of food we ate, some prisoners used the rest room only once a week. They took joy in keeping the papers as their only possessions. Number 92 kept many of her toilet papers and presented them to me.

"This is the only thing I can offer you."

To show her my gratitude, when I received them I counted, "One, this is your heart; two, this is your love; three, this is your treasure; four, your service; five, your beauty." I counted all the papers and thanked her for them. She turned away from me sadly.

"I am a bad woman," she said.

"In the eyes of Jesus, we are all sinners. You and I are the same." I went on to talk with her about Jesus Christ and how He died on the cross to save us. "The worst thing we can do," I said, "is to forsake God."

Her eyes were sparkling, which showed that she really understood me. When she admitted that she did wrong and repented, the truth touched her heart. From then on, when I taught her the Bible she sat quietly in reverence.

"Miss Ahn," she said one day, "would you please ask Jesus to let me go to hell? I would like to be near my husband. I want to apologize, and I want to suffer with him. Not knowing he was going to hell, he was killed by me. I sent him there. Now I want to comfort and love him. Please, ask God about it."

"I understand what you are saying," I told her. "But your husband chose the way he would walk. When a traveler travels, no matter where he goes, he goes home. Those who listen and obey Jesus will go to heaven. Those who do not know Jesus will not go to heaven but to their own place."

She had another favor to ask of me. She wanted her date of execution quickened.

"When I think of my husband who is in hell, the thought torments me. If they do not execute me, I must kill myself in order to go to my husband."

Her determination was alarming and I felt a great burden to pray for her.

The day of her departure arrived, and three male jailers came for her with handcuffs and ropes. When they called out her number, she saluted me with her two hands on her forehead.

"Thank you very much," she said calmly and with assurance. Serenely she left the cell and held out her hands for the cuffs. They did not have to use the rope on her. She walked ahead of them, as though hurrying to meet Jesus Christ.

Without wiping the tears which were streaming down my cheeks, I watched her depart. Without fear, she put death aside and walked. It was exactly as when Jesus conquered death.

"Death is swallowed up in victory. O death, where is thy victory? O grave, where is thy sting? The sting of death is sin; and the power of sin is the law: but thanks be to God, who giveth us the victory through our Lord Jesus Christ" (1 Corinthians 15:54–57).

29

THE
SCABBED
BABY

One day a pregnant woman was brought into our cell. She had been living with her husband in the mountains and valleys. In the spring, their food supply had diminished, and starvation became a reality. Because of her pregnancy, she often fainted from hunger. Unable to endure seeing her suffer, her husband stole a cow, killed it secretly, and sold it to buy grain. They were caught, and she was imprisoned for conspiracy.

Because she had fought extreme poverty since birth, she was not an ordinary woman. Her hands looked as hard as stone and as strong as iron, for she used them in place of farming tools. Her face was blunt, and both her voice and speech were so coarse and abrupt that one could hardly tell she was a woman except for her pregnancy and bound hair. Her scab-covered body looked horrible, and she was continually scratching. A few of the other prisoners already had scabs, and the periodic washing and changing of prison uniforms seemed to be spreading the scab disease throughout the prison. In the evening everyone tried hard not to sleep beside prisoners with scabs because they scratched their bodies until they bled. No one, therefore, wanted to sleep by the new prisoner.

"Don't worry, everyone," I said, "because I'm going to sleep near this lady." I led her to the back and slept beside her. Since there were so many of us, we had to sleep like packed sardines. And because of the cold, we all slept holding one another's feet against our bodies. This naturally caused the scab disease to spread to all the prisoners. The new woman scratched her body throughout the night, so I was unable to sleep at all.

One morning several days later she gave birth to a tiny girl. Hurriedly I called a jailer and she went to the office and brought back a few pieces of blue cotton cloth. The mother's uniform was soiled from giving birth, so the jailer changed her clothes while I wrapped the baby neatly with the blue cloth and then put her on her mother's bosom. Although the mother tried to nurse the baby, it was so frail and weak from the severe cold that it never opened its mouth. Taking the baby, I removed the cloth and put her naked body against my bosom. Little by little the baby began to move. Because of her extreme malnutrition, she was very tiny, her head being only as large as an adult's fist. Her legs were only skin and bones, and her tiny body was covered with scabs. She was unable to cry, but her cold body was moving.

Although the mother was bluish purple and shaking from the extreme cold, nothing special was given her, not even a cup of hot water. She tried pressing her breasts, but not a drop of milk came out. The next morning some cold gruel was given her for the baby. Leaving very little for her child, the mother swallowed the gruel as if it were water. I put the remaining gruel into the baby's mouth, but she didn't seem to have the strength to swallow it, although her mouth moved a little.

While holding this scabbed baby on my bosom, I was pondering over many things. I had been told that when I was born, I was so tiny and weak that Father kept me alive by holding me against his bosom. I was probably as tiny and miserable as this baby. However, as I thought how happily and lovingly I had been raised, I was thankful to God. At the same time, I prayed with all my heart that God would have mercy on this tiny life. Then I thought of a name for the baby. I decided on Okja, explaining the meaning of the character Okja to the child's mother.

"Okja, or whatever her name will be, she will soon starve and die," the mother replied. It was true. Would there be any way that we could help this infant live? As I looked at her resting on my bosom, she was opening and closing her tiny black eyes. But having no strength, she was unable to cry and could only wiggle her arms and legs now and then. As this tiny child wiggled, I felt a love for her arising within my heart. Little by little she ate the watery gruel. Awake or asleep, all my attention was centered on this precious life.

I asked God to look after this poor infant. But on the afternoon of the eighth day after her birth, I noticed that her breathing was suddenly becoming difficult. Very soon she was immobile and in critical condition. The tiny body stretched out momentarily, and then it became cold. But still she looked sweet, as though she were sleeping peacefully. I showed the cold baby to her mother, and she turned her face away. I saw she was about to weep, but she did not shed tears. Her blunt face revealed the pain of hunger rather than sadness. A male guard came, and the dead baby was taken away.

Okja lived only for a short time, but what a happy and beautiful tiny flower she had been! For eight days, without seeing the rough world and without being touched by the evil of men, she was on the bosom of a prisoner. Although she had opened her eyes, she had not seen any of the misery of human life before dying. Had I died long before, I would not have known this suffering and hunger, but I realized that I had my own mission. I was given a burden from God, a burden to fight and die for His name. Someday, I knew not when, I would like to die beautifully like Okja.

After that, a scab started to spread vigorously on my chest.

Even in between my fingers, scabs had developed which made me feel unbearably itchy. The more I scratched, the more unbearable it became. From scratching so hard, I was bleeding all over my body. The scab started to spread among all the prisoners in my cell. It was frightening to see everyone scratching herself uncontrollably. Everyone was now groaning from the pain of scratching. I selected Scriptures which were God's promises and explained them to the others in the cell. Then we decided to pray with one heart. The scabs gradually started to heal and soon they were gone, leaving no scars.

Through this experience the prisoners began to fear the Lord and His words. At the same time, we had great joy. While showing our completely healed hands and bodies to each other, we all thanked the Lord and rejoiced together.

Although the tiny baby had brought the scabs and had left us hurriedly, yet by means of the scabs that she had left, God had given us faith and great joy.

30

THE GEISHA SUN WHA

Sun Wha was a well-known Geisha. Pretty and fluent in Japanese, she had been favored by many high officials. Many men loved her but she was not attracted to any of them until she met a grammar school teacher. She had been living luxuriously, and when the teacher moved in with her, he quit teaching. He became the leader of a group of opium smugglers and made a lot of money. However, his smuggling activities were discovered and he and Sun Wha were arrested, along with his men.

When Sun Wha was first brought to prison she was very arrogant, complaining bitterly about the food and being treated like a prisoner.

"I'm not afraid of you!" she stormed at the jailer. "A poor jailer is like a dog! How long are you going to keep me in this pig house? You fool!" Then she directed her abuse toward her mother, whom she seemed to resent greatly.

She pushed and shoved at the rest of us so she would have room to move around the cell. She didn't know what she wanted, except to be released. She was soon clamoring for a cigarette, alternately pleading with the jailer and berating her. With an attitude like that, the other prisoners began to abuse her.

On the evening of the next day I started to sing a hymn rather loudly.

"That song is lovely," Sun Wha said, listening. "And so is your voice."

I told her that I had taught music at a girls' high school and had memorized 150 songs. I sang another for her, and as we talked afterward I asked her which part she liked the best.

"I can't repeat the words because I've never heard that kind of song before. But I was so moved that I felt like crying. Would you sing that again?"

When I finished all the five verses of one hymn, Sun Wha asked if I would teach her the song. First I had her memorize the words, a task which she was able to complete quickly. After repeating the melody a few times, she was able to sing with me.

I admired her patience and tireless attitude. At last she learned all the songs by heart, singing the hymns as if she had found a rare treasure. However, when she talked with others, it was always about passionate love between men and women. She spoke openly about the men with whom she had lived. Finally I asked her to stop.

"Now I want to tell you something very important," I said. "Would you please listen to me?"

At first she seemed offended, but her attitude changed and she listened.

"Once there was a tremendously wealthy man," I began. "All he had to do was change his luxurious silk clothes every day and eat the extravagant food the cook prepared for him. But outside the gate of his house a beggar waited. When the servant gave the leftover food to the dog, the beggar always shared it. Since the beggar had no home of his own, he slept in a dirty corner of the town. As a result, he had a skin disease and wore dirty and miserable clothes. Unable to buy medicine or go to the doctor, he finally died."

I went on to tell her that the rich man also died and had an extravagant funeral. But he went to a terrible place of burning fire after his death. The flames could not be put out, and when he could endure them no longer he thought about the times when he had spent so much money only for himself. He had never thanked God.

Then he saw the beggar who had always eaten what the rich man had left outside the gate of his house. But the beggar looked very happy and peaceful in the arms of a nobleman. The rich man saw that the nobleman was his ancestor, Abraham, and he called out to him for help.

"Please have Lazarus carry a drop of cold water here to cool my tongue."

"There is a great chasm that has been fixed between you and us to prevent anyone from crossing from where you are to here," Abraham replied.

Then the rich man asked that Lazarus be sent to his house to warn his five brothers so they could avoid coming to the place of torment. But Abraham told him there were many in the world who teach plainly about heaven and hell. There are churches, pastors, evangelists, and many other Christians who fervently teach about them.

"No, Father, when I was in the world, I mocked the Christians and would never listen. But if someone would go to my five brothers from the dead, they will all listen and repent."

"No," Abraham said. "However fervently they might be taught, those who have no ears to hear will never hear, even if someone would rise from the dead and tell them."

I went on, then, to tell her about my own imprisonment, explaining in detail how Jesus, the only Son of God, came to earth as a man to save us sinners. I told her about the suffering He had to go through for the ransom of our sins.

She listened intently, her large eyes wet with tears. She continued to memorize hymns one after another and then began to learn Bible verses. She was completely made anew. How greatly she had changed from the arrogant girl who first came to our cell and was continually crying for a cigarette.

"I'm truly a sinner, Teacher," she said to me. "I must return my husband to his wife, shouldn't I? I'm already determined to do so, though it makes my heart ache to think of having to live without him. When he wasn't with me even for an hour I felt as if I had been in a desert. How will I ever be able to part from him forever? I can only cling to God. Oh, what should I do? My heart aches."

As the days went by, her resolution became noticeably stronger. One day she talked to me seriously.

"I'm thinking of visiting his house as soon as I'm freed. I want to apologize to his mother and wife and to be forgiven by them. Afterward I want to go into some mountain village and build a church where I can preach to the villagers and teach hymns to the village children."

From then on she prepared her mind toward that goal. The jailers no longer abused or mocked her. Seeing her gracefulness and sacrificial behavior, one jailer commented that she was very different.

She also witnessed when she had the chance. "If you return to God, He will give you joy, peace, and blessings," she told her new friend. "Having your sins forgiven is the greatest gift you can ever have. You'll only suffer loss if you don't believe Him."

At times when we became too hungry to be cheerful, I would have her teach me the ancient Korean dance and we would both dance together. She would often fast for three days, during which times she either forced me to eat her meals or else gave them to others.

"Teacher," she said to me, "we are hungrier than Lazarus, but we'll never need to be regretful like that rich man. We'll be happy as can be forever, won't we?"

On another occasion she told me that she had never truly loved anyone. In a way she loved her common-law husband, but he had his legal wife, which caused her heart to burn with jealousy.

"I was constantly thinking of committing suicide, either

alone or with him," she said. "I never had a day that was truly happy or peaceful. Now I really love you, Teacher. I see how wonderful it was for me to have become a prisoner."

Not long after that she told me about a disturbing dream. She said her husband had peeped in the window and told her good-bye. Then he disappeared to a faraway place. Even in her dream she had remembered her resolution not to attempt to follow him.

That afternoon a jailer came in to tell her that her husband had died. Soon after that she was sentenced to a year and was taken to the prison factory .

She changed into a red prison uniform and lingered in our cell reluctantly. When she finally had to go, she bowed to me three times and wiped the overflowing tears from her eyes with her hand.

"Will you not forget me?" she asked. "I shall surely be beside you in heaven forever."

Turning away, she disappeared toward the factory with the jailer. To my eyes soaked with tears, she looked like an angel in red. What a beautiful reborn child she was!

31

THE NURSERY
IN THE PRISON

A country woman and a very thin little boy were brought to our cell. Her husband had quarreled with another villager and became so angry that he set fire to the cornfield of the other man. The woman was arrested for standing watch while her husband burned the villager's crop.

The woman was thin and nervous, and the boy was gaunt and bloated from malnutrition. He was so hungry and frightened that he was shaking violently. He became the center of attention in the cell. For some reason, when he saw me he held out his arms to me. Holding him tightly, I could not help shedding tears.

"You are such a good boy," I told him. "And this auntie is a good auntie, so do not be afraid."

The mother said she called her son "Stone."

"That is not a very good name," I said. "Why don't you call him Un Suk [Stone of Grace]."

"Call him what you please."

While holding Un Suk on my lap, I was filled with endless thanks. But what could I feed this child? How could I relieve him from the misery of prison life? While I held him, he fell asleep and slept so long and well that we all began to worry about him. And when he woke up, he didn't glance at his own mother but stayed on my lap. After several days the mother was sentenced for three years and had to go to the prison factory. While Un Suk was in my cell he never cried, but when he was taken to the factory he cried all the time. They tried hitting him to make him stop crying, but that only made him worse. Finally he came down with a high fever.

"He might stop crying if you take him to cell one," his mother told the jailers.

They brought him to me, and he held up his hands and threw himself upon me. I talked to him softly, telling him to stop crying, which must have seemed strange to the jailer because I was crying myself.

The prison doctor came to examine him and told the jailer that Un Suk should not be confined to a cell. "He's not a convict," he said. "Let him go out into the sunshine to play as much as he likes."

However, they could not allow the child outdoors alone. Besides, he would not leave my side. Following the doctor's orders, the chief jailer commanded that Un Suk and I should both go outdoors to play in the sunshine.

"Is it for the sake of the child or someone else?" the chief jailer mocked. "Before women, men become frail. After all—"

But her attitude did not change the situation, because the doctor outranked her and she had to follow his orders. I knew what the jailers were saying, but I was happy to have a chance to be outside with Un Suk. The severe winter had already gone and the air was full of the soft and gentle breezes of spring.

My heart melted into thankfulness as I realized that the Lord had provided me with such pleasure. Around this time a new Japanese jailer with a very cute daughter was employed. Because her husband had died in the war, she got permission to work in the prison and to bring along her three-year-old daughter. Yoko, her little girl, had a sweet round face. She, too, became attached to me without any hesitation. Holding her arms out, she asked me to carry her on my back as I did Un Suk.

Although she was not very heavy, she felt as heavy as lead to my body which was weakened from malnutrition. Yoko's mother confided that when she had taken her daughter to the chief jailer at the time of the new shift, the child had shrunk from her.

"Mommy," she said. "I'm scared of this auntie!"

So she started leaving her daughter with me. Yoko would dash for my cell on the days her mother came to work, demanding that Un Suk and I come out quickly.

"I feel assured that Yoko loves you so very much," her mother told me. She had already told me something of her agony as a widow and about the terrible chief jailer who was like a viper. "Yoko calls you 'Auntie, Auntie' while she hates that old fox and those dirty, malicious jailers. But they can't do anything to me. As a war widow, the law protects me from them."

When the time came for the prison warden, to inspect the female ward, the place was in an uproar. The chief jailer stood in front of all of the prisoners and commanded us to clean up the entire ward. She even called in the convicts from the factory who cleaned up the dirt in the yard, the corridors, and from every corner. They wiped and polished all the windows and washed the floors.

Meanwhile, with noisy footsteps and the clacking of sabers, the warden and other officials appeared. Everyone was in uniform. The warden behaved as if he were a king ruling over the 5,000 prisoners and the many officers. When he saw Un Suk, he asked if he was the child who had cried so much that he became sick. The chief jailer said that he was.

"Do not treat him cruelly," the warden said. "Take reasonable care of him."

The prison doctor glanced at me and smiled. "How is your prison life?" he asked.

"It's not too bad," I told him.

Just then Yoko came running to me and was calling out for me loudly, "Auntie, Auntie, Auntie, come out quick and play with me."

For a moment the situation was tense, but the warden seemed to understand and approve. He ordered the door to the cell opened, and Yoko flew to my arms. Her tears stopped. "We need a baby-sitter," he continued. "Let the three play as they like." On the way to the next cell, I heard him talking to himself. "A merciful Buddha, I see. They say one who is loved by children is never wicked."

Finding an unexpected humanity in his speech and attitude, I could not keep from smiling. God had been working for me. Carrying both Un Suk and Yoko on my back, I went out into the yard, where I looked up into the sky which was as beautiful as it must have been when it was first created. The flying birds were glorious. I felt like calling out to tell them of God's love.

> Then washed I thee with water; yea, I thoroughly washed away thy blood from thee, and I anointed thee with oil. I clothed thee also with broidered work, and shod thee with seal-skin, and I girded thee about with fine linen, and covered thee with silk. And I decked thee with ornaments, and I put bracelets upon thy hands, and a chain on thy neck. And I put a ring upon thy nose, and ear-rings in thine ears, and a beautiful crown upon thy head (Ezekiel 16:9–12).

I thought the Lord had done for me exactly what these verses described. But most of all I memorized verses from the Gospel of John. In every phrase and verse I put myself in the grace of God as though I were directly listening to His voice.

I often considered the last verse of John's Gospel which told that the world could not contain the books that could be written about all the things Jesus did in His lifetime. That had bothered me and I had asked my mother about it, wondering if John knew how vast and infinite the universe is.

"Although man cannot measure the universe," she said, "Jesus is greater than the universe because He is the only Son of God, the Creator. John could write the last verse because he fully realized this truth."

At the time she spoke, I understood with my mind. Now, however, I understood with my heart. The love of the living God is greater than the universe.

Un Suk and Yoko brought me great joy. As I played hide-and-seek or laughed and talked with them, I would completely forget that I was in prison. I taught Yoko many songs and dances, and she would memorize them very quickly and sing the songs with me. Un Suk would imitate Yoko by moving his lips and trying to dance. Whenever I sang hymns, the children made all sorts of noises. They didn't understand what I was singing.

I was endlessly happy in the prison. I sang hymns and prayed aloud, asking God to bless these two children. I also resumed my calisthenics that I had not done for a long while. Thinking I was dancing, the children would try to imitate me. I would burst out into hearty laughter and even the most wicked jailer was not able to stop me.

But the situation was not to last. The chief jailer of our ward seemed unable to watch my enjoyable life. One day she came out to the yard and glared at us.

"Men are stupid!" she shouted.

I knew well enough that she was talking about the warden and the doctor. Before long, Nakamura took Yoko with her to the prison factory and Un Suk accompanied them. Once more I was confined to my cell where I would recite Scripture and meditate day and night.

32

HEARTY LAUGHTER

After losing both Yoko and Un Suk, I was feeling extremely lonely. But I realized that Jesus loved me far more than I loved the two children, and He protected me and made it possible for me to be happy, even in prison. He never asked me to do anything difficult, but only to believe and trust Him.

One morning jailer Kuriyama came to the cell and told the jailer in charge that she was to let me out to meet someone. I was overjoyed to see Kuriyama after so long a time.

"That old fox couldn't tolerate seeing you so free," she said softly. "And the jailer standing by the cell is said to be quitting soon because of illness. She says you pray so much that the prison is different than it used to be.

"Anyone who dislikes you either becomes sick or has to leave for one reason or another. She says the prison is becoming like a kindergarten. Not only that, but she says that all of the men from the warden to the judges have fallen in love with you and allow you to do whatever you like."

"That should be headline news," I murmured.

"As for me," she went on, "I will do nothing but follow you."

People who probably were the families of other prisoners were looking at me anxiously as I went into the meeting room. I was overjoyed to see Mother there. My heart froze momentarily, however, as I looked at the stern faces of the inspector and the male jailer standing nearby.

I sat straight across from my mother. While I was hesitating about what I should say first, she suddenly spoke out loudly, like a primary schoolchild reciting a phrase he has been forced to memorize. *"Oganke desuka."*

She meant to say *"ogenki desuka"* which means "how are you?" in Japanese. Since the regulation stated that no one was allowed to meet with a prisoner unless the visitor spoke Japanese, she must have learned those few words from my sister. Instead of asking me how I was, however, she had said, "lid of a toilet bowl." She didn't realize what she had said, but I couldn't help from breaking out into laughter.

"Kyah!"

I knew I shouldn't be laughing, but I could not stop. The harder I tried, the funnier I felt. My laughter grew higher and higher in pitch until it reached my highest soprano. In an effort to speak, as the given time would soon expire and my mother would feel guilty if she were rebuked or abused by the inspector for my action, I bit my lips in an effort to stop. At first my eyes were completely closed as I laughed, but finally I was able to glance at the inspector. He was hiding his face behind some paper, and by the way it was shaking I could tell that he was also laughing. So was the male jailer who stood beside him. Kuriyama was laughing, too. That made it even harder than before for me to control myself.

My stomach and both ends of my lips began to ache. My chest hurt from the laughing, and tears were brimming in my eyes. Still, I had no power to stop laughing. The time allotted for the meeting must have expired, but everyone except my mother kept on laughing. The male jailer was laughing so hard that he sounded like a monkey.

"Dear," Mother said, "would you please stop now? You've laughed enough."

I was still laughing as I left the office and said to my mother who was following me, "Mother, you needn't worry about me. I'm so happy, even able to laugh as much as I have today."

"Whatever might happen to you," she cautioned me, "you should never forget the moment when you shall reach the gate of heaven. Be faithful," she said.

I felt like a seriously sick patient because of my painful stomach. The inspector said to my mother, "I want you to say *'Oganke desuka'* again the next time you come to meet your daughter, Mother."

His words made me overjoyed, for he had called a prisoner's mother "Mother."

Still laughing, Kuriyama said, "I've never laughed so much in my life. In this world, you can't find laughter anywhere."

My heavenly Father had given me the joy to laugh. Because He is always close to me, I can rejoice. The Lord had made me laugh until nothing could stop me. I could laugh for eternity. Today I am the happiest person in this present, troubled world!

33

TORTURED FOR SINGING

The happiest yet saddest time for those of us in prison was supper. We were happy to eat, but the moment we finished we were even more hungry. One evening as we finished eating we were surprised to hear someone singing a hymn so loudly that it resounded throughout the entire ward. The song was coming from cell five. Jailer Fujita, who was in charge, went to the cell and ordered the new prisoner to be quiet. But that did not stop the singing. Fujita struck the singer ruthlessly on the head with the large key she carried.

"What is God?" the guard demanded. "I'm not afraid of your God, you mad fool!"

The newcomer was praying aloud, praying that God would intervene. Over 3,000 Christian churches had been closed for having refused shrine worship, and many pastors had lost the power of the Holy Spirit because of the confusion and harsh torture by the Japanese police force. This prisoner was appealing because the Kingdom of God had been profaned. She was calmly and fearlessly praying to God, entreating Him for the 400,000 Korean Christians who were unable to hear the Word of God and had been dismayed like strayed sheep by hypocrites who had turned out to be spies. Then she prayed for the martyrs dying under the cruel torture of the Japanese military police force and for those believers' families who were starving to death.

My heart was about to break, I had to lie down and cry out to God. Even while I was praying, the thought frightened me that the big key she had been beaten with might have badly injured her. I was unable to sleep. What should I do if Mrs. Choi would worship tomorrow as loudly as she had today and if Jailer Yagi treated her as cruelly as Fujita had treated her?

The jailer who was to be in charge the next day had a reputation as bad as that of Fujita when it came to battering the prisoners who did not please her.

"Jesus," I prayed, "give me the courage Mrs. Choi has. I'm in agony because of the torment she is going through. With Your power and holy love, bring a solution to this urgent problem. Give me faith like hers or make my nerves insensitive."

The time for the new shift came and another jailer took over, but it was not Yagi. I stared at her in amazement. She saw that I was looking at her and came over to me. "You must be the person," she said. "You must be the famous lady."

I was irritated by her words, for I thought she was mocking Mrs. Choi by what she said.

"Call me Number 57," I told her.

"Oh, no, not Number 57. They say you can talk with representatives and generals quite fluently and that high government officials become dumbfounded before you. All the male jailers say such things. They say there is a character in the female ward and that unless we are extremely careful, we'll get badly teased."

She said she heard I was being imprisoned for not worshiping the shrine and that she thought it was crazy to confine people for such a reason. I felt that I had to warn her that such talk could get her into trouble.

"If I get into trouble," she shrugged, "I'll quit."

What she said made me concerned for her, but she was far better than the malicious and cruel jailers such as Fujita and Yagi.

The young jailer was my companion in whatever she talked about. She was on duty during lunchtime. When the meal was served, Mrs. Choi's shrill voice singing hymns rang through the ward. The new jailer ran to her cell to stare at her in amazement.

"What's the matter with her?" she asked me when she came back.

Since I was unable to answer her immediately, she went to cell five again. When she came back, she spoke quietly: "This morning the chief told us to report anything unusual that takes place. I wonder if she meant about her in cell five."

"She is worshiping God," I said.

"Does her God like to have her sing so loudly against regulations?"

"She has probably always worshiped in that way. Or, perhaps she may be demonstrating to others that God is the Head and the highest above anything. That's the truth, and she is a wonderful Christian."

"You are a Christian, too, aren't you?" she asked. "Why don't you act like that?"

"Perhaps I do not have faith as strong as she does," I said. "I'm a very weak, cowardly person."

"That's not true. It can't be. She has her ideal. You have yours. But what should I do? What would become of her if I reported what she is doing?"

"She would be tortured," I said.

"I shall not report her then. If they blame me, I'll just say that I didn't know."

I thanked God for this girl. However, I was still very uneasy. Too many prisoners liked to tell such things in an effort to gain favors for themselves.

The next morning Fujita was on duty, and I waited anxiously. Just as I feared, Mrs. Choi's worship fell at the time when the cruel guard was on duty. Fujita sent for the chief female jailer and a male jailer from the office. Together they dragged Mrs. Choi out into the concrete corridor and put handcuffs on her, confining her hands behind her back. They opened her mouth and forced her to bite a thick stick braced across her mouth which they tied with a rope. Then they stuffed her mouth with dirty pieces of rags until she was unable to make a sound. The rag in her mouth soon was stained scarlet with her blood. I expected her to fall to the floor at any moment and to die and be received in heaven.

I decided to fast. I was unable even to sleep. It was as though I were roaming in hell alive, and I became completely worn out. Fujita seemed to take fiendish delight in torturing Mrs. Choi. It was obvious to me that she would not be satisfied until she saw the devout woman's corpse.

The next day when the jailer came out of cell five, she was completely exhausted. I didn't know what she had done there, but it was obvious that she had lost her strength. She sat down on the cement floor and the jailer who was to take over the next shift asked her what was wrong.

"My legs are as weak as cotton," she said. "I can't stand up."

She was unable to walk alone, but with the other jailer's help she was finally able to leave the ward. She was never seen in the prison again.

According to the jailer, Fujita had acute tuberculosis and was sent home to die. The wooden stick and the handcuffs were taken away from Mrs. Choi. The rag was removed from her mouth, and she was given a meal.

The hymns and prayers that were heard three times a day from cell five were hoarse and weak, yet once she started to sing, the entire ward became solemn. The jailer in charge only waited silently for her to finish.

God lives!

34

A BEAUTIFUL
SWINDLER

One afternoon a young woman was brought to our cell. She had smooth, white skin, a modern hairdo, and sat elegantly. I was captivated by her fresh, polished beauty and was glad that she was in with us. Sensing that I was sympathetic toward her, she sighed deeply.

"Number 12," I said to her, "you must have experienced hardships to be sent here."

"Even if I talk about them, nobody believes me, so I don't want to talk," she said.

When suppertime came she said that anyone who wanted her food could have it. The other prisoners took it and divided it among themselves.

"Do you really like this chicken feed?" she demanded. "I want to throw up just looking at it."

"This chicken feed will turn into grains of gold for you one of these days," one of the others reminded her.

After supper she told us that she had grown up in a church and was a Christian. She spoke with such determination that I believed what she said.

After graduating from one of the more important girls' high schools in Pyongyang with a straight-A average, she had married into a wealthy family in the city. Looking as though she was about to start crying, she related how a detective had approached her husband and herself in a famous restaurant in the city and arrested them on suspicion of having a dangerous ideology.

While we were talking, jailer Kuriyama returned. Since Fujita had been discharged because of her illness, Kuriyama was assigned to our cell again. She took everyone in our cell out for exercise. While we were in the inner courtyard she warned me about Number 12.

"She's a notorious swindler," she whispered, "and has been convicted four times."

It was hard for me to believe that, and I thought there must have been some mistake. Number 12 sensed the change in my attitude. When the three-minute exercise period was over and we returned to our cell, she wanted to know what Kuriyama had said about her. I tried to pass it off, but she seemed to know that the jailer had told me that she was a swindler. She claimed the story had been started by the detective who arrested her. He wanted to make love to her, she explained, and when she refused his advances, he started the tale that she was a swindler.

"The jailers make judgments just by reading the report," she said, kneeling and starting to cry. "I feel disgraced and frustrated."

During the night she told me she was pregnant and craved candy. Her mother used to tell her that a baby would be born blind if a mother didn't get to eat the things she wanted to while she was carrying him.

I cried, too. When I thought of an innocent baby being born blind, my heart was in agony. Kuriyama heard our crying and voices and looked in. Number 12 listened to us talking.

"You and Kuriyama seem to be good friends. She is so kind and understanding and beautiful. Didn't God send her here for you?"

"I think so."

"You will think I'm presumptuous," she continued, "but if you ask Kuriyama, she will listen to you. You are a devout Christian. Don't you think it would be cruel for my baby to be blind for the rest of his life?"

I had to admit that bothered me a great deal.

"You could help, if you would. If you ask Kuriyama, she wouldn't say no. She would buy some candy for you."

"But that is against the laws of the prison," I said. I held the same attitude about the civil law that I held for God's laws. But now an innocent life was about to come into this world, and it seemed to be appealing to me for eyes.

I asked the Lord for His help and also talked with some of the other prisoners. They were all opposed. "You can't trust her," they said. "If you do, you will be in great trouble."

A middle-aged swindler looked down at Number 12 contemptuously. "You are a cunning fox," she said.

When Kuriyama came again, Number 12 once more implored me to get her some candy. Although I resisted for a time, in the end I told the guard about Number 12 being pregnant and her strong desire for candy.

"So you want me to buy candies at the black market?" she asked. "Is that it?"

Feeling melancholy, I waited for Kuriyama's next duty, but Number 12 seemed to be happy. When the jailer came and called the roll without giving me any candy, Number 12 became irritated. Again the older woman who was awaiting trial for swindling warned me about her.

"I know her kind," she said. "You will lose your reputation if what you are doing becomes known."

Much later that night Kuriyama put the candy through the meal hole. I gave it to Number 12. Not even thanking me, she took it and ate it without offering me a bite.

Wha Choon, a girl on the death roll, was wide awake. "She ate it all herself," she said miserably.

I tried to console her by reminding her that there would

be far better things than candy in heaven, but Wha Choon was crying and I was crying too. Number 12 had fallen asleep after eating all the candy and I still did not know whether I had done a good or bad thing.

The next morning Number 12 ordered me to ask Kuriyama to get more candy for her. "But this time I want rice cake."

The next time she was on duty, Kuriyama brought a big rice cake which Number 12 again ate all alone. I thought she had gained confidence because she knew now that her baby would not be born blind, but her gentleness seemed to disappear. Again she ordered me to have Kuriyama buy her more candy. I refused, and her attitude changed completely.

"Don't you know that you ordered the jailer to buy candy?" she asked. "Because of this you are going to be handcuffed and tortured until your bones are crushed."

As if I had plunged over a thousand-foot cliff, everything was dark and my body was trembling. The next moment I came to my senses. As I looked up to the Lord, I stood firmly and asked His help. He filled my heart with strength.

"Number 57," she said coldly, "order Kuriyama what I tell you to, or you will be handcuffed and tortured."

I closed my mouth and did not respond. The other prisoners were so stunned they could say nothing. But they raised their fists and were ready to beat her.

I decided to fast. When I began, Number 12 snatched away my meal and ate it.

When roll call came that evening, Number 12 called Kuriyama aside and said arrogantly, "When you come to work on your next shift, you know what you have to do. I will only withhold reporting you today."

Jailer Kuriyama did not yield. "Let her report it," she said quietly.

When Number 12 realized that everything was not going as she had planned, she became outraged. She kicked and beat older prisoners and spat on them like a mad woman. The others became afraid of her. Although our cell was small, it had been called a chapel of heaven, but now it was about to become a demon's den. At roll call time the next morning, Number 12 told the chief jailer that she wanted to report something in secret to her.

Although the time was short, the other prisoners and I prayed to God. After a while, each prisoner was summoned, one by one. None returned. At last I was called in. My heart was completely calm and I had a feeling of gratitude.

Jailer Kuriyama was also in the room when I got there. I did not see any of my prison mates, except for Number 12, who was kneeling on the floor. The chief male jailer demanded to know if I knew the law. I said I did.

"Yet you broke it," he said. "Why?"

I told him about Number 12 being pregnant and worried about her baby being born blind, so I had appealed to jailer Kuriyama who knew the feelings of a mother.

"But I have come to know how cruel it is to break the law," I said, "because I have been threatened by Number 12 every day."

"Did you eat any of the candy?"

"No."

"What about the rice cake?"

"I ate none of that, either. When I received it from Kuriyama I handed it to Number 12, and she ate it all."

"Did anyone else eat it?"

"None."

"Were the other prisoners sleeping?" the chief jailer asked.

"I thought they were, but when Number 12 was eating the candy and the rice cake, everybody was sighing and crying."

"Why didn't you eat it?"

"It was not my food," I said simply.

Then he turned on Number 12. When she admitted that she had eaten both the candy and the rice cake alone, he began to lash her furiously and mercilessly with a thick leather whip. I turned my back and tried to cover my face with my hands to blot out the terrible thing that was happening.

All of the other prisoners except Number 12 were returned after questioning. She was placed in a single cell which was a torture room.

But she fought back, blaming Kuriyama and me for her troubles and scheming to get even with us. She made friends with the chief female jailer and the bad jailers. The bad prisoners were also on her side. A great deal of scheming and plotting went on in the prison between some of the guards and a certain element among the prisoners.

Number 12 conspired to steal wool and silk from the prison factory and have it sold through the black market on the outside, a scheme which required the help of both the bad prisoners and the corrupt jailers. She was able to bribe her way out of the torture room and be put in cell six.

She never seemed to sleep at night; she was always busy doing something secretly. We could smell the good food she had in her cell. Food was more important than life. It was easy to bribe prisoners with food. Those who tasted the black-market food changed. They spread their smiles to Number 12 and served the bad jailers as though they were queens. But the gentle and good jailers and prisoners protected me.

Consequently, the women prisoners were divided unofficially into two groups. The two jailers who were on the side of Number 12 were terrible women, and in that group were swindlers and thieves.

Her plan soon became plain. They would have jailers Kuriyama and Jue fired in order to harass me. I decided these experiences might be God's will. Hunger, trials, and unbearable tribulation provided good opportunities to experience the Lord's promises. The entire attitude of the prisoners in the women's section changed. The wicked got their way, while the Christians were apprehensive and fearful. It was possible to tell which group any woman belonged to just by looking at her.

We could not escape from Number 12, nor could we dissuade her. The bedtime trumpet sounded in derision. I felt as if I were buried in a grave thousands of feet deep. Although I had extremely poor blood, I fasted for three days. My body seemed to dry up, my breathing was constantly painful, and every time I coughed it felt as though a needle was being driven through me.

"If I quit," Kuriyama said, "you won't have a bad time like this. But when I quit, what will happen to you? I want to stay here and come to see you every day."

After a few days I realized that we should wait for the Lord to act. *He will make everything better soon; He will teach me through this situation,* I told myself. *I do not know the world of evil, so that's why He is showing me all of this. He will soon judge everything, so be cheerful and wait.*

One day an incident that shook the entire prison occurred in the women's section. A wool company brought a large amount of wool to the women prisoners' factory. A silk factory was asked to manufacture huge quantities of silk cloth at the prison factory, so the prisoners knitted sweaters and shawls of the wool, and kimonos and bedding from the silk. The bad jailers, along with the bad prisoners, bribed the guards at the main gate to let them take silk, silk cloth, and wool materials to the outside.

But their plans went awry. One guard was summoned elsewhere for duty, and a guard who could not be bribed took over. He caught the thieving jailers, and the prison was in a tumult. Authorities swarmed into the women's sector to inspect the factory and question the prisoners. But none of the bad prisoners spoke well of the bad jailers.

"They would harass us if we didn't give them what they ordered," they said, "so we did as we were told."

Many of the bad jailers were discharged immediately when the entire story came out. It was even revealed that they had bribed certain prisoners with food and had cruelly treated the good prisoners.

In addition it was proven that they gave false reports on jailers Kuriyama and Jue. The bad prisoners were moved out from a good cell into a bad cell. Number 12 was discovered to be the chief conspirator. When that evidence was presented, she was handcuffed and placed in a special isolated cell. Jailers Kuriyama and Jue were each awarded a pair of shoes and were triumphant.

The Lord lives and judges.

35

A YOUNG GIRL CONDEMNED TO DIE

Although she was only sixteen, Wha Choon was exceptional. She seemed completely worn out from being detained at a police station for so long. Her girlish face was as pale as a pumpkin blossom, and there was a large scar over one eye. Nothing seemed to interest her. At first I thought she was anxious about being in jail, but I was not prepared for her increasing nervousness as night approached.

The other prisoners were annoyed with her and pushed her to the corner where the toilet was. She acted as though she wanted to move to the center of the cell, for it was just below the window, but the regulation was that a new prisoner in a cell had to sleep near the toilet. At midnight when the footsteps of a jailer on watch approached, she suddenly got up and began to whimper plaintively.

The other prisoners rebuked her, and the prisoner next to her even hit her with her fist. Quickly I went over to her and lay down in the place nearest the toilet.

"I don't mind the cold," she said in response to my question about it, "but I'm scared to death. My husband follows me wherever I go. In the evening he peeks at me through that window. And he stands up in that corner, too. Oh, I'm so frightened!"

I grabbed her hands and said in a low voice, "Don't be. Nobody is there. Let's pray to God and ask Him to cast out the evil spirit," I said. "He will always help us if we pray."

Both she and I got up together. She waited on me in complete trust. "I believe in Jesus," I continued. "If we pray to Him with all our hearts, believing that He will help us, any demon or ghost shall flee. Do you understand?"

"Yes," she said. She still did not seem to fully grasp what I was trying to tell her, but she seemed to be relying on my judgment.

"O Jesus," I prayed, "save this young girl from the hands of the evil spirits."

Still holding my hands tightly, she looked around at the corners of the cell and then up at the window. Her expression was stiff at first, but gradually it became relaxed.

"You can sleep now," I told her, "because we prayed."

I lay down beside her. She always slept doubled up, she said, because she had never had a quilt. It had become her habit to hold her knees when it was cold. I could well imagine what extreme poverty she must have experienced.

Tears of thankfulness washed my face. There was no other suitable way for a human to express this joy except by crying. The cold, my strongest enemy, attacked my body, chilling me like ice, but I would still keep on singing for joy.

The wind coming through the big hole in the floor penetrated my flesh, making the pain brutal. I cried out within myself. Then I began to feel warmth coming from the girl's body. Her cold feet were becoming remarkably warm. Without my knowing it, I had fallen asleep. I had intended to help her, but instead I was being helped by her.

Several days later I came to learn that she was deeply troubled at the thought of facing death. Every time she heard a jailer coming, she thought the time had arrived for her to be taken out to be executed.

"Try not to worry about it," I told her. "I may be executed with you. Why don't we live together as close friends and die together?"

She seemed to be greatly comforted by what I had told her, and at last she was able to approach me without any reservation. I found that being the same kind of person had a special effect on her. That was what Jesus had done for us. He became a human being like ourselves and walked among us. If He had not become a man, He would not have been able to save us.

In the days that followed she told me her whole story. While she was a baby, her father had carelessly dropped a pair of scissors on her, which had caused the terrible scar. The people in her village claimed that the scar was the sign of murder, and she was even shunned by her own parents.

When she was thirteen a stranger came to her village looking for a bride. When he could find no one else, he took Wha Choon, promising to give grain to her parents. Her husband had been so cruel that she fled from him repeatedly, only to be caught and beaten and sent back to the fields again. He forced her to buy liquor without giving her any money for it, and she was so miserable that she tried to take her own life a number of times.

After two years she met Chun Soo, a boy who had been her friend before her marriage. He and his family had moved to a neighboring village, but he had heard how unhappy she was since her marriage and wanted to help her as much as he could. He often went to visit her as she hid in the cornfield.

He was the one who gave her the strychnine she used to poison her husband. He had been using it to kill deer, and she talked him into giving her some, saying that she wanted to get rid of the mice around her home. She was sure her friend had given her the poison to kill her husband, but when she told him what she had done he reported her to the authorities. She was arrested just when she was beginning to experience Chun Soo's tender love. Now she was condemned to die.

"I shall love her," I promised God. "I must lead her to Jesus and see her overwhelmed with His love so that she may know true happiness."

The only way I could show her my love, I decided, was to give her my meals. However, determined as I was, all the food went into my mouth when it was served. What a despicable, ugly person I was. I was upset and sickened at myself. I rebuked and insulted myself more than I had ever done before, but when mealtime came, I was again finding excuses. The battle continued for several days, but each day I lost. Then while I was praying, a ray of light touched my spirit.

Within my heart I cried, "Now I shall offer my meal to Jesus! I shall offer it to Him and allow His will to be done!" My heavy heart became lightened and refreshed.

I carried my food quickly to Wha Choon. "This is Jesus' meal," I explained. "I have offered it to Him. And He wants you to have it, so thank Him and eat it."

At last she began to eat. She ate my lunch and supper as well, without fully understanding why. For the next two days she ate the rest of my meals.

"Well," I said, "are you getting less hungry?"

"Yes, but how about you?"

"These meals were all from Jesus. I have given them to Him."

"Why?" she asked.

"You need not worry. You don't have to ask about anything. We are doing fine." I could not help crying with joy.

Some of the other prisoners blamed Wha Choon for my tears and accused her bitterly.

"She has been treated badly all her life," I told them. "Why don't we be nice to her while she is with us? Since I don't know when I'll be executed, it's more fun not to eat at times than it is to eat. Look! Don't I look happy?"

I wondered if I had ever experienced the worth of being a human being so much as now. It was an unbelievable privilege for a person like me, sinful, selfish, conceited, and with many faults, to receive an order from God, who was the Lord of the heavens and earth. I was overwhelmed. In spite of my weakness and sinfulness, the Lord had given me the grace to walk and work with Him.

Wha Choon began to weep, but now she was crying because of love. The joy of being loved touched her so deeply that her tears flowed freely. I told her many Bible stories in a simple manner so she was able to understand them. Again and again I repeated the same stories, asked her questions, and made her tell me what I had said.

She seemed to like the Old Testament story of the harlot Rahab who had hidden the spies and had been saved because of it. Day after day I told her about the women of the Bible. As her interest grew, her eyes would shine like a child's when I told her the same stories. I tried hard to help her understand how compassionate Jesus was. When I saw that she was beginning to memorize, I attempted to have her learn John 3:16, explaining each word to her. Then I began to teach her hymns. I sang the hymn by Isaac Watts she seemed to like best a number of times every day.

> Alas! and did my Saviour bleed? And did my Sov'reign die?
> Would He devote that sacred head For such a worm as I?

She was finally realizing its true meaning with her entire heart and being.

One day she started to fast. I did not think she would continue for more than a day, but she fasted for four days, continually reciting John 3:16 and crying her heart out while singing hymns. It was not the cry of despair but of heartfelt repentance. On the fourth day I asked her why she fasted so long.

"I only fasted three days," I told her.

"Because I am so sinful I added one more day."

After she finished her fast, she looked like a brave soldier. Although she was weakened physically, she looked more confident.

"My lover, Chun Soo, is innocent," she said one day. "How do you think I can save him?"

"The court will call you for a hearing," I said. "You must tell them clearly that you deceived him in order to obtain the poison. Do you think you can?"

"Unless I tell the truth fully, I shall be unable to die without regret."

She often fasted for three days. I was unable to change her determination. Her round face became thin and pale, and the scar seemed to have shrunk. Her nose was also becoming straighter, and she was indeed becoming a pretty girl. The jailers and other prisoners began to love her.

In the evening when she returned to our cell after being called to the court, she looked happy and proud.

"Teacher," she said, "I told them everything. Jesus was helping me, for I was able to speak so fluently. I told the judge that since I have become a Christian I cannot tell a lie. I fear sin more than death. I said that I can hardly bear the agony of the lie I told about Chun Soo."

It was a miracle that this illiterate girl could have been so brave and eloquent before the judge. I could not help praising the Lord with all my heart. He had chosen the ignorant to humble the wise of this world.

She was a completely different person. Her tears had dried and she laughed vivaciously in all the loveliness of her youth. Faith shone in her face.

When I saw her waken before dawn and begin to pray earnestly, I asked her about it. At first she only smiled, but when I pressed for an answer she told me.

"I can't stand it to see you cough so much. I've been praying that Jesus would let me have your cough."

I felt my eyes grow warm and moist. "O Lord!" I prayed. "How can I praise Thee and sing of this beautiful love?"

She looked so happy that the others in our cell envied her. "I wish I could laugh like she does," one of them said. "I would like to experience fun like that just once."

As I listened to the prisoners talk about her, I felt very thankful. Jesus was able to make even a condemned convict truly happy.

Very early one morning she woke me to say that she had had a very strange dream. For prisoners, a dream carried a grave meaning. Something extraordinary was about to happen. On some occasions it was something good. On others, it was something bad. Usually the clue was in the dream.

"I was in very long and beautiful snow white clothes and was flying in the sky higher and higher and forever."

This must be the day her death penalty would be executed, I reasoned.

"Let's get up and worship together," I said to her.

We began to sing a hymn softly. Together we recited John 3:16 and we prayed. As we were finishing our prayer, we heard footsteps approaching our cell from the end of the hallway. All the world in front of me darkened as if the dawning sky had suddenly retreated into night.

"Thank you for everything, Teacher," she said in a trembling voice.

"You know who Jesus is, don't you?" I asked her.

"He is my Savior." She started to cry but told me that she was not crying for herself. "I'm crying for you. I cannot help it as I think of how much longer you must suffer here."

Oh, how courageous she was as she went toward the scaffold! She looked as if she were proclaiming that she was walking with Jesus. In overwhelming emotion I talked to the Lord about her.

"Jesus, she is another beautiful re-creation of Yours. How happy I shall be when I see her in the place of our eternal home with You!"

36

HANDCUFFED!

One morning the male jailer came in and called my name. The sky seemed abnormal and foreboding as we walked to the court. It was the color of copper, and the air was thick and heavy. The atmosphere was dark and eerie, as though the earth had just stopped trembling from a great earthquake.

"It's a strange day," the young jailer said in a low voice. "I have never seen the sky this color. It seems that a catastrophe is about to happen. Is God angry?"

When we arrived at the court, it was in an uproar.

"We did it!" one of the officers said exultantly. "We finally did it! We attacked Pearl Harbor and declared war on America! Their entire fleet is destroyed."

"Now it's our turn to rule!"

There were no trials that day. We prisoners were sent back to our cells.

A week or so later I had a bad dream and awakened with a heavy feeling of oppression. My nightmare was clear. Under a huge old tree a large, dark blue poisonous snake was coiled, its eyes fixed on me. I was terrified but, calling on the name of Jesus Christ, I cut the snake in two with a sword. But now there was life in both ends of the snake. Both were ejecting venom. Loudly I called upon the name of the Savior and slashed the snakes in two again. Once more they doubled and there were four poisonous snakes attacking me.

When morning came I learned the meaning of my dream. The chief woman jailer called the roll and ordered us to worship the emperor as the living god by turning our heads to the east.

I did not do it.

"Just see what will happen!" she threatened me.

Leaving the cell, she returned moments later with a male jailer, a torture instrument, and handcuffs with iron chains and knots. The other prisoners were taken out, and I was left alone in the cell.

"What's the use of rebelling against those mad dogs?" the male jailer whispered to me as he handcuffed my hands behind my back. "Let them do what they want."

As time went by, the heavy iron knots and chains bit deeply into my bony torso. Eating with the handcuffs on meant that I would have to eat like a dog. This was something I could not do. When the meals were brought in, I turned my head away from them.

As the days went on, my entire body was burning with a fire that would not be put out. A sharp knifelike pain plunged down my neck to my breasts and my shoulder. My eyes, my mouth, and my nostrils were aflame. I fainted, but it was only a matter of seconds before the burning and dreadful, relentless pain came back.

The unbearable pain was the pain of hell.

I recalled the dream in which the eyes of the poisonous snake were staring at me. I had to fight this pain by relying on the Holy Spirit. "O Lord," I cried out. "Stand up and fight for me."

I was half dead and unable to pray. How happy I would

have been to die! I would have run quickly and caught death by the hand if I could have. But this merciful release was denied me.

The nights were long. Each second was like a day, and each day was as a year, passing slowly.

It was difficult for jailers Kuriyama and Jue to see me being tortured in this way. They also refused to eat, and they cried for me; but there was nothing they could do.

I don't know how long the torture continued, but eventually word raced through the ward that an important guest was coming. Not long afterward I heard the sound of a man's footsteps coming to my cell. It seemed that he was at my cell for a long while, staring at me. I kept my eyes closed and hoped that he would not see my face. Finally the footsteps left.

"O Jesus, please remember me!" I prayed. Sorrow engulfed me, but I was unable to cry.

"Lord," I told Him, "I am a woman, and this torture is harder than the cross. It has lasted for days. Please hurry to me. Hurry, O Lord."

I didn't know if I would be crippled or insane. I didn't care. I only wanted to be saved from the constant goading pain. Why didn't I die?

I pleaded with Him to take away my senses and to let me die. Surely if I had been a strong Christian a miracle would have occurred to take away the pain, or I would have been given the strength to bear it calmly. In my desperate prayer I was complaining. Realizing my weakness, I became afraid. I thought I had faith, but did I really have it or was I just deceiving myself? Would Jesus forsake such a sinful person? Was I a valueless, sinful child, of no concern to God? I was confused. Because of the excruciating pain, I could not recite any Scripture.

"O Lord," I continued, "I am a woman. This torture is too long. It is cruel. Since a woman was made from Adam's rib, she is only one-twelfth as strong as a man. Remember this, please, my Lord. Hurry to me!"

The next morning a man came back to my cell and un-locked my handcuffs. I shouted and fainted. Jailer Jue was there with me, massaging me, but I was unable to open my eyes.

"If I were God," a male jailer blurted out angrily, "I would send them down to hell."

"It would be deserved," Jue answered tearfully.

The prison doctor examined me. "That witch of a chief jailer really hates you," he said. "I don't see how you can still be alive." He took my pulse. "Her pulse and breathing are the same as those of someone who is dying," he commented.

I was already half dead, and the prospects of living dimmed my eyes. In that moment I thought that this life was my strongest enemy. I was forever a failure. I was weak and only partially alive, but I was unable to die. My flesh did not seem to know how I longed to end the battle to live.

My enemy was the idol worship of imperial Japan. I could not avoid the ruthless power of the military forces and the po-lice unless I died. When I was released from the irons, I had a high fever, and it was many days before I was well enough to eat the prison food. Under the doctor's orders, soft, watery rice was given to me. According to Kuriyama and Jue, the chief jailer was furious when she got orders from the judge to un-lock my handcuffs.

"Is he also in love with that woman?" she demanded. "And that doctor! He should mind his own business."

When jailer Jue told the doctor what she had said, he turned to me. "She will try to get revenge on you again, but don't worry. You have beautiful spies working for you." I knew he meant my jailer friends, but Jue only shrugged her shoulders.

Even though my high fever lingered, causing dizziness and dehydration, the love of God gave me strength and cheer.

During the middle of the night I was awakened by Jue, who handed me a can filled with cooked warm rice. "Where did you get it?" I asked her softly.

"One of the male jailers stole it from the kitchen and told me to cook it for you. Everyone knows that you were handcuffed."

I took some of the rice and put it into my mouth, but it was difficult for me to eat it because I was so moved by their love. I ate every grain of rice and offered thanks to God. *What a splendid and joyful experience on this side of heaven,* I thought. Even if I had died that instant, I was the most fortunate person alive!

37

DESPERATE
HUNGER

The prisoners sent to the women's ward from the police station increased in number day by day. Having so many in each cell made it easier to resist the cold, but our breath changed into steam and fell on us like snow. A wide variety of people were being admitted. A pickpocket, a drug addict, a fortune teller, a whore, the madam of a brothel, an arsonist, a gold smuggler, a murderer, and a counterfeiter filled our room. Some cursed their fate angrily. Others cried, lamenting their imprisonment. I was among the trash of society. I was also one of them. This made me giggle.

The professional pickpocket who was put in with us looked relieved to be back in prison. She had been convicted four times and would undoubtedly receive a sentence of five or six years, but she didn't seem to be disturbed by that possibility. Some time after she was brought to our cell, she took an old belt made of cowhide from her waist. We were amazed to see it, knowing that every new prisoner had to go through an inspection in the nude. We didn't see how it had been possible for her to get it by the guards. She tore off a piece and chewed it. Some of the others wanted to try it, too.

The pickpocket tore off pieces of the leather with her teeth and distributed them to the others. Chewing did seem to soften the belt, and the prisoners appeared to be content. I had not held out my hands, so I wasn't given any leather.

"A great teacher like you wouldn't like to eat dirty stuff like this," the pickpocket said contemptuously.

Tears of regret filled my eyes as I realized that I could have had a piece of leather too if I had simply extended my hand. Covering my eyes as if to pray, I made a firm resolution. When I was finally released I was going to buy twenty fresh leather belts, cut them, and chew them all day long.

"Miss Ahn is praying in tears," one of the prisoners observed. "So chew more softly."

She didn't know that my contradictory feelings frustrated me. Eventually the belt was gone, for they had eaten it all. For the first time since the pickpocket had produced the belt, relief swept over me. A thief's goods should not be eaten, I told myself. I was glad I had not eaten any of the stolen goods.

In this way I comforted myself.

Our hunger ripened to despair, but my reliance on the Lord was complete. One day after roll call, the change in the jailer's shift brought us a new jailer. She had a royal bearing, and I surmised that she did not need to work to earn money. Moreover, she had a kindly look about her. I asked her why such a beautiful person as she would come to a place like this to work.

"I am neither beautiful nor pretty," she told me. Lowering her voice, she went on. "My husband is Higashi, section chief of the fuel department of the country. I know Sheriff Kuga and other high-ranking officers. Those who know you well always talk about you. You are very famous."

"I'm an unusual prisoner in that I am trying not to commit a crime," I said, "but I certainly am not famous."

"Since my husband has to go to the war, I can't live just by staying at home. Anyway, if I have to work, I want to be near you. I talked it over with my husband. He agrees that I should leave our one-year-old son with my mother-in-law so I can be here to help you."

Could this be possible? It was indeed another miracle. My heavenly Father was the same as an earthly father who does good things for his children.

"When I was a child," Mrs. Higashi said, "I heard that in prison there are good people as well as bad. Many outstanding politicians and government leaders were once in prison."

The two of us became good friends. She brought a bagful of salted crunchy Japanese cookies and gave them to us. It was like a dream. And when night came, she brought us delicious rice balls.

"Mrs. Higashi," I said, "I can't believe this. It's like a dream."

"Even when I am at home," she told me, "I can think of nothing but the cell. My husband is eager to hear what I tell him. Mother packs things for me to bring here. Everyone is interested in you."

She brought the prisoners in our cell many kinds of food, which we ate quietly so that nobody else would know what was going on.

"If necessary, I'll bring more," she told me.

"What will happen when the chief woman jailer finds out?" I asked.

"Don't worry about it. I give her something she likes every day, too. I also give things to the other jailers, so don't worry."

My body was getting thinner and had become bent into a stooped position. I was not able to stretch, and felt paralyzed. All my strength was gone. It was hard to move even one finger, and opening my eyes was not easy. Even conversation got on my nerves.

For obeying God's law I had been confined in prison. I had a sudden craving for apples, but I could not get even one and I wondered why. Those who disobeyed the Lord not only had apples but were able to eat to their hearts' content. But here in prison, I could not even eat the rotten beans and decayed millet they gave us. The smelly and unnutritious soup was made of weeds and looked like dirty water used for washing feet.

However, my desire for apples became stronger. "O Jesus, I would like to eat an apple," I prayed honestly. "You know my body system. You are the only One who can cure this painful desire. Please grant me one whole apple."

I could not help but think of apples. If I had a fortune, I thought I would be glad to give it up for one whole apple. But if somebody were to bring me a barrelful of delicious apples and say, "Eat them and worship the Shinto gods," I would have kicked over the barrel and said, "I don't need them! I don't need them for the rest of my life!"

"O Jesus, You must be planning something wonderful for my future," I prayed, "please give me one whole apple, even if You have to give up the plan. Maybe it is impossible because of the time and place, but You satisfied 5,000 people with five loaves of bread and two fish. Now I must really depend upon Your promise. You said that You would grant every desire which is asked in Your name. Trusting Your promise, I am praying." After praying, the pain that had twisted my nerves began subsiding somehow, and an indescribable warmth filled my heart.

One day during the change of shifts I overheard jailers Jue and Kuriyama talking. "At this time of year, apple rations are being distributed, but all the apples are rotten. Maybe the section chiefs have taken the good ones."

When I heard them, I jumped up in my excitement. The word "apple" made my mouth want to water, but no saliva came. I called to Jue immediately. "Mrs. Jue, is it true that apple rations are being distributed? How many do they give?"

"How many? Why?"

"Mrs. Jue, don't you see our food? It's nothing but decayed, smelly things. Rotten apples are much, much better than what we're eating every day. Can you get those rotten apples?"

"Now I know what you mean."

"Will you get them for me?"

"Even though they are rotten?"

"I don't mind. I want to eat those rotten apples."

"All right, that's easy to do. I'll bring them to you."

Hearing this, I was so happy that I almost danced and jumped for joy. When Kuriyama came for the change of shifts, I asked, "Mrs. Kuriyama, you are going to give us apple rations today, aren't you?"

"Apples? You mean those rotten, mushy, soggy apples?"

"Yes, please, get those rotten, mushy apples for me."

Jailers Kuriyama and Jue went for the rations. Many of the other jailers did not want the rotten apples, so Kuriyama and Jue each received a bagful. As the night advanced, Jue brought the soggy apples and put them through the meal hole one by one. Oh, what an aroma of heaven! I was so overwhelmed by the fragrance that I almost fainted. "O Lord, this aroma is sufficient!" I prayed. "How splendid it is! God still lives. God is the God of promise."

I praised God and worshiped Him with all of my heart. As soon as I got hold of an apple, I put it into my mouth. It was like an apple that had been boiled. It was so soft that it melted in my mouth right away. *The fruit in heaven must be like this,* I thought. The hard, frozen apple, melted by the warmness of spring, had become juice. A tap on the apple would produce juice. Every prisoner ate at least one. Wha Choon and I ate a lot of them. What a wonderful world it was! The prison became a paradise!

Jailer Kuriyama brought us a lot of apples in a sack too. Wha Choon and I ate them all. My stomach, shriveled and dehydrated, was filled with nutritious apple juice, like a soft spring shower poured onto a dry lawn during the night. The ache that had been piercing my body stopped, and my entire body functions recovered. Even my twisted nerves calmed down.

"What a wonderful world God has created!" I exclaimed. "Oh, what a wonderful prison this is! What a lofty road of the Lord! O Lord, You are faithful to Your promise. I will tell this to people in heaven and the world."

My waist straightened. I could use my voice again. I explained to my fellow prisoners why God gave me soggy apples instead of firm, smooth ones. Because my teeth were weak, I wouldn't have been able to bite into a firm apple. I had to add that God had given me fifty apples instead of just one because my dehydrated body needed many soggy apples rather than one fresh apple which I could not have chewed. The apples were truly tasty, and their sweetness and delicacy were the best that I had ever tasted.

The next day, one of the prisoners, looking seriously at me, wiped away her tears. I asked her why she was crying. "I have always eaten good food, but I never acknowledged it by thanking God as you have, even for rotten apples." Then she wept even more, and I cried with her for joy.

38

FATHER'S REPENTANCE

During my long period of imprisonment I seldom had visitors. For that reason I was surprised one day when I was told that a visitor was waiting for me. My sister had come to tell me that our father had died.

"He was saved," she said. During his two years in the hospital, he completely repented of his sin. He kept asking where he would be going after his death, and just before he died, he repented.

"He kept calling your name and he asked Mother's forgiveness. For ten days he cried for the sins he had committed, but when he was ready to die he called upon the name of Jesus, repented for everything before God, and praised Him."

The visit was only for three minutes, so she spoke quickly and left before the jailer stopped us.

Back in my cell, I kept thinking about Father. When I was born I was so small and thin that the relatives ridiculed me.

Father looked down at me. "Poor baby," he murmured. "They say you are not like a human. Don't die, but be a great person."

Father took concubines in accordance with our custom and the advice of his parents, and they gave birth to many boys. Each time a concubine child was born, he was registered as Mother's child. But Father paid the most attention to me, and when I became old enough to go to church I once had a chance to talk to him during suppertime.

"Father," I said, "would you believe in Jesus and go to heaven with me when we die?"

"God is for the poor," he told me. "Your father has everything. It's not necessary for him to go to church."

One day my Sunday school teacher said to me, "Your mother will be all right; she will go to heaven. But your father will go to hell, pounding his heart and not believing Jesus as his Savior."

I knew Father's life was sinful, and this worried me a great deal. When I saw him at suppertime I could not keep from crying. He was surprised and asked me what was troubling me.

"Mother and I will go up to heaven," I told him, "but you will be going down to hell. This makes me cry."

"I don't know about Jesus or church or even hell," he told me, "so I don't believe in them. But when you say that you will go up and I will go down, this is something I have to think about."

After Mother left him, he tried to get her to come back, but she would not. After that he started drinking and did not return home for a long while. He went to China, Japan, and Manchuria. And when he returned home, he was old. When I was about to visit Tokyo to give the Japanese a warning from God, I visited Father and told him that I might be killed because of the proclamation of God's command. He sighed and tried to stop me, but I was not going to change the decision of my heart.

"I admire you," he said. "Man cannot live for righteousness unless he is great."

"Father, I'm your daughter," I replied, "so I implore you,

please return to God." I gave him the big Bible I had prepared especially for him and asked him to read it.

Now Father, realizing his lost condition, had cried for his sins and had called upon the name of Jesus in repentance. Finally he had surrendered to God.

My prayer was answered! How thankful I was that God had heard me!

39

THE GOVERNOR'S
SUDDEN DEATH

In the early days of the war with the United States, Japan was sure she was going to win, even as she had won the war against Russia. There were troubling developments, however. In an effort to conceal the inner turmoil, the Japanese authorities planned to increase the power of the Shinto spirits by persecuting the Christians.

The defeat of the Japanese in the seas to the south made them worried, even as shortages of raw material plagued them. Everything made of iron was confiscated and presented as a gift to the government to make guns and arms. Everyone from grade school children to college students was being forced to learn and to practice how to kill American soldiers by the use of bamboo and wooden sticks.

One day jailer Jue brought me the newspaper telling of the latest directives as soon as she arrived at my cell. She had the paper of the previous day. The article she wanted me to read said that at 9 A.M. on the eighth day of every month people under the domination of Japan, regardless of age or sex and including prisoners and the sick, must worship

Japan's god, Amateras Omikami, and the other eight million Shinto gods, for the success of World War II. The general public was ordered to the shrine, while the sick and the prisoners were to worship in the direction of the shrines. Every state governor would lead and perform the worship ceremonies. The eighth day was chosen because the Japanese armed forces had attacked Pearl Harbor on the eighth day of December. (In America it was still Dec. 7, but for us it was the eighth day because of the difference in time zones.)

I looked up to the Lord with sadness. Just as King Hezekiah had taken the letter of the Assyrian king into God's house and opened and read it, I did the same. I spread the paper on the floor and prayed.

"Heavenly Father," I said. "Read what is written on this paper. Please read what it says about the imperial conference. I am in fear, O Lord."

The next morning Kuriyama told me that all the jailers had been called together and told about the new order.

"This is a serious matter," she said. "Those who refuse may be slaughtered."

It was Satan's plan to get the Asian people to bow to the gods of Japan. Just as King Nebuchadnezzar had built the golden statue and forced people to worship it, the Japanese rulers were doing the same thing. My strength gone, I almost collapsed to the floor. Darkness covered my future, but in the depth of my heart there remained a firm and indescribably beautiful purpose. Opening my burdened heart, I prayed for strength.

The chief jailer knew me well enough to know what I would do. She moved all the prisoners out of my cell, leaving me alone. Determined to fast, and now all alone in the cell, I did not talk. The rushing fear was strong enough to make me give in, but I had to go on.

The powerful enemy was the country of Japan with its cruel power and eight million gods. I had no reputation, no power, nothing. Then how would it be possible for me to fight? I would fight with the aid of the legions of angels from heaven. Without eating, drinking, speaking, or sleeping, I fasted for three days. My nerves were as sharp and keen as a razor's edge. The sound of a flying insect sounded like the bugle of the enemy. The opening of a door was like enemy gunfire and almost as unbearable. Again and again I tried to recite Psalm 91.

The eighth day finally came. As usual, the rising bugle sounded, but the time for the change of shifts of the jailers was long in coming. I sat in silence, waiting prayerfully.

Fear threatened me like some terrible storm.

"O Lord, I am too weak," I prayed. "I'm a sinner. I deserve torture. I remember Your many miracles and how You healed me. I heard Your voice clearly, but now I am afraid of the torture that will be coming."

No work was being done in the factory. All was quiet.

"What time is it?" I asked jailer Higashi.

"It's 8:35." She was as worried about me as I was concerned about myself. Twenty-five more minutes. I would be walking through the valley of the shadow of death. I tried to recite the Scriptures, but my efforts were not successful. Fear caught the words in my throat. I looked up at Jesus on the cross and felt as if my heart were being crushed.

Only five more minutes, I thought. I had such weak faith. Real faith would not be as frail as mine. My bones already felt as though they were broken, and my blood was hot and pounding through my veins. My neck felt as if it were being pushed up by some irresistible force.

Was I a fool?

The pastors and elders I had seen at the Pyongyang police station had been calm and composed. Their faith was as solid as a rock. Why was mine like a grain of mustard seed? My faith was like a small butterfly in a storm.

"It's 8:59" Mrs. Higashi said, although I had not asked the time. My heart was like a sword piercing me with cold, flashing fear.

"It's 9 o'clock."

My heart fell. Mrs. Higashi's voice was husky, but nothing happened. Neither the siren nor the footsteps of the male jailers was heard.

"It's five after nine," Mrs. Higashi told me.

Was I dreaming? In disbelief I stood.

" Are you sure your watch is right?"

"It always keeps the correct time." She looked down at it. "It is now 9:08."

Something must have gone wrong. But what? Was the siren out of order? Had the governor overslept? Or had someone made an error in the time?

Mrs. Higashi went to the office and checked the time, but it was the same as her watch. Twelve minutes after nine.

"Why didn't the siren blow?" I asked her.

"Because you prayed so hard."

"And why didn't the chief woman jailer or the other jailers on duty show up?" I wanted to know.

"It's because you fasted and prayed."

"Please," I said tautly, "don't make fun of me."

"I'm not making fun of you. You are different."

The tense prison was completely silent, so quiet we could hear the sparrows clattering busily outside. After ten o'clock the gate was finally opened, and people began to come in. When jailer Kuriyama appeared I asked her what had happened. But I couldn't wait, so I asked Mrs. Higashi to find out what had happened at headquarters and to come back as soon as she could. I had no right to order her around, but unlike me, she was mature and not offended.

Kuriyama told me that the people were gathering at the square and that the commandant had begun to speak when the phone rang. The commandant was interrupted and he went to answer the phone, but he didn't come back. Finally one of the officials dismissed the crowd.

The officers on duty would tell Mrs. Higashi nothing. She brought that word to us and then went to phone her husband to see what he could tell her. About thirty minutes later she came back with the shocking news that the plane on which the Isaka governor was a passenger was missing.

"It hasn't been found yet, so that's why the conference resolutions were not carried out."

I knelt and prayed, "O heavenly Father, You have shown me that You are the Savior. I was about to be devoured by the lion, but You saved me from its teeth. You are the living God. You are the blessed God who does not forsake the trusting child. You are the Creator. I adore You. I fear and love only You. I will listen to and obey You forever and ever."

My words were so inadequate that I felt the need to recite Bible verses. I recited psalms and praised Him with all my strength.

Mrs. Higashi brought more definite news. After the conference, the Korean governors were returning on the plane. While it was still over the Sea of Japan, an American fighter plane appeared and shot it down.

The Japanese attempted to kill my soul with the resolution of the imperial conference. They didn't know that I was in the hands of the Lord.

> Because he hath set his love upon me, therefore will I deliver him: I will set him on high, because he hath known my name. He shall call upon me, and I will answer him; I will be with him in trouble: I will deliver him, and honor him (Psalm 91:14–15).

40

MY
SISTER'S
LOVE

I could never forget my sister's love for me during the long period I was in prison. Without her support it would not have been possible for me to endure. Since I could do nothing to help Mother, I was comforted by the fact that my sister was taking care of her.

When my sister was young she was easily the most beautiful woman in town; therefore, she was greatly sought after and was married to a rich man. Although she had all she could ever want of material things, she cried a great deal because her husband was not faithful to her. From her abundance she bought the finest of clothes for Mother and me.

I had a habit of giving away my old things when I was given something new, a fact that disturbed my sister. "I chose the best for you and had it made especially for you," she would say. "You don't understand me."

I may not have been very considerate of her feelings, but I would often give away my coat to someone I felt needed it worse than I did. And when the two of us were together, I would occasionally ask her to give away something she was wearing. She would comply with my request reluctantly and often grudgingly.

"You were the thief in our family," she told me, secretly proud of my generosity. "You carried everything to the poor. We thought you were crazy, but Father always said, 'That girl will amount to something.'"

"Because of you my purse is empty," she told me on one occasion, "and only you will get the reward."

We enjoyed each other's company and had a good time spreading the Gospel. She often asked me what kind of a man I wanted as a mate.

"He must be a good Christian," I said, "an engineering graduate, tall, and someone who loves music and possesses a clear bass voice, and a person who makes money and spends it and does not complain. I want a man who is affectionate and has a sense of responsibility. He must be understanding and willing to go out with me to spread the Gospel by distributing tracts."

"Is there such an ideal man in this world?" she asked.

Strangely, many love letters came for me from many men I knew, and from some whom I had never met. Mother's command was that I was not supposed to read those love letters, but that didn't bother me because I had no interest in reading them anyway. But my sister opened and read them. She seemed to enjoy it.

"You blushed," I teased her. "You look as though you are in love."

"I wish I could have received two or three of these letters before I married," she said. "How happy I could have been. Just once I want to be loved passionately."

She lived with the truth now. She had joined the line of the martyrs. I am grateful that she dwells in my heart as one of the most beautiful women in the Lord.

41

REJECTED
FREEDOM

My health, especially my eyes, deteriorated as the months passed. During the winter they seemed to be frozen and were filled with mucus when spring came. I wiped my eyes with my hands, but the mucus kept coming, and I could not see clearly. Although I was not particularly sad, tears constantly flowed from my eyes.

Kuriyama and Jue were both quite concerned about my eyes. I knew my eyes were getting worse, but that was of little concern to me because I was still sure I was going to die. However, the kindly jailers reported my condition to the prison doctor, who came to examine me.

"Your eyes are bad," he acknowledged, "and your feet look frostbitten." He shook his head.

Kuriyama was the one who brought me the news that I might soon be released from prison.

"But I would not have much joy in working at the prison anymore," she concluded, "if you weren't here."

The doctor had informed the court that if I was not released and treated soon, I would go blind, so they were considering some sort of special action.

I was frantic with excitement. Was this to be possible? Could I be with Mother? Then I remembered my gratitude and deep emotion when I was sentenced to death to join the ranks of the martyrs. I had felt it was an honor and a privilege to be a Christian. If I went home, even because of the eye disease, I would lose this honor. Was I falling into the devil's trap? A sudden chill of sorrow passed over me. I wanted to live with Mother in this world, and my ardent dream was about to come true. But had I not already discarded this? I worried about it all night. When morning came, my decision was up to the Lord.

The next morning my cell was opened, and I was ordered out into the hall. Jailer Jue accompanied me. "You are free!" she said exultantly. "You are going home!"

I felt as though my feet were not touching the ground. She was saying something, but I was too excited to listen to her. From the iron gate and iron chains I was going to be freed. I was so happy I wanted to sing aloud, yet a heavy uneasiness nudged me.

I looked up at the heavens. What a wonderful sight!

Seeing Mother standing in the small office, I ran and embraced her. I felt as if I were at the gates of heaven, but she was not excited. In fact, she acted rather cold. I wasn't expecting her to be like that. Although I could not see clearly, I could tell that she was not looking at me. I broke out in a cold sweat.

"Mother!"

"Why are you coming out from here?" she demanded in a tone that revealed she was not happy about my homecoming. "Why should only you receive such a privilege? Other believers do not come out."

"My eyes are bad. If I don't get treatment for them, I will go blind. That is the reason they have ordered me to leave."

"Do you think the people who sentenced you to death have that kind of concern for you? Then why did they intend to execute you?"

"God did this for me."

"Many Christians are dying," she said, "but you can come home. I don't understand."

"I'm not completely free," I told her. "At home, good food in a warm room and plenty of rest will cure me. When I am cured I will return to prison."

"Do you think you can get nutritious food these days?" she persisted. "And where can you find a warm room? Everything is rationed now. We can get nothing except by rationing. Not even a grain of rice. The Japanese say that Christians are traitors, so we have to eat bean husks, leeks, or anything we can get. Because of these, I am blind now; I can't see your face.

"No matter how cold it gets, we can't get fuel. My feet are so frostbitten that I can hardly walk. A citizen who is loyal to God has no place in this world. Christians in prison are dying, and so are the believers outside."

Her words slammed into me savagely. "I was a fool," I told her. "I didn't know." I couldn't cry, even though I wanted to. It was as though there was a knife in my heart!

"Why do you worry about your eyes?" she asked. "Didn't you give everything to the Lord, including your eyes?"

I came to my senses. I realized now that I was not my own anymore.

I was deeply touched by Mother's words. This great teacher of faith had brought me up and was ready to be martyred with me. I thanked her with all my heart.

"I understand everything now," I said. "You are a great teacher for me. Please do not worry about me. Eyes are not important. Let's stand up and fight." I turned to the head of the department and the jailer and said, "Please let me go back to my prison cell."

"I have never seen anything like this before," the senior officer, who was a Korean, said. "The daughter is great. The mother is greater."

Cheerfully and briskly I went out of the office and walked toward the women's prison. Strong, courageous music rang in my heart. A sacred symphony seemed to be soaring from my heart to the sky and returning again.

"Mrs. Jue," I said, "in my heart I'm singing a great hymn. May I sing out loud?"

"If you don't sing too loudly," she said.

But the high, beautiful notes would not come out. I gasped for breath, unable to continue one stanza with a voice too hoarse to make more than a few feeble sounds.

Supported by Mrs. Jue, I walked in front of the office of the women's prison, where the chief woman jailer looked surprised to see me. We went on to my cell. My cell mates were surprised to see me again, but I didn't have the strength or interest in telling them why I had returned.

"You'll understand later," I told them.

I was exhausted like a balloon with the air escaping. Wanting to give strength to my heart, I recalled passages of Scripture. Savoring the joy of being whole in spirit again, I knelt and prayed, thanking God with deep awe and emotion.

That night I drifted off into a restful sleep. From the next day on, my eyes were upon the high red brick wall. Mother had said she came down every night to the wall and prayed for me. I could see her standing on frostbitten legs, looking up at the heavens and praying for her daughter. Her body was merely skin and bones, like a winter tree that has shed its leaves. Yet, every night in that severe cold she stood at that brick wall and prayed until daybreak.

I had seen many splendid things in my life, but never had I seen as pure and as graceful a lady as she. My mother was a saint created by God, and I, her daughter, could not endure the persecution she had gone through. I wished that either she or I would be called by the Lord and die as soon as possible. That was the only way.

"O Lord," I prayed, "call Mother first if it is Your will that we are called at the same hour."

It was comforting to know that my older sister was with her. In order to keep her faith, my sister had forsaken fortune and prosperity completely and was joining the martyrs by staying with Mother. My sister must have been waiting outside the gate. If my eyes had been normal I could have seen her.

THE ROCK STANDS UNCHANGING

Quite unexpectedly the court ordered me to set my thoughts of prison life on paper. I thought it must have been in preparation for the death penalty. For some reason I thought I would be held in prison for ten years before my life would be required of me. It was now more than five years since I was first arrested. I was grateful that the end was near. Embracing death with thanksgiving and deep gratitude to my Lord, a new exhilaration swept over me. Even though I had been sinful and unworthy beyond measure, Jesus loved me and was concerned about me.

Few people, except for my mother and sister and a handful of Christians, knew or cared whether I lived, but in death I would be following those great saints of God who had already died in prison or had been executed. A host of angels and pastors, including Chae, Lee, Joo, and the others would eagerly welcome me.

I had no regrets for my long imprisonment. Life had been wonderful! Death would be even more marvelous! As soon as I entered heaven, I would sing a hymn of praise, thanking the Lord.

I wrote this poem in Japanese and handed it to the jailer who was standing in charge:

> The solid *Rock*, in an ocean expanse,
> The billowing waves, crushes,
> When it compels the *Rock*,
> Yet the *Rock* stands unchanging, everlasting.

"Is this your essay on your impressions?" she asked curiously.

I told her that it was, and she would understand it when she read it. She went over it two or three times but said she could not grasp my meaning. I could have explained but I did not.

Although I knew my trial was imminent, several weeks passed before I was called to court and taken to the judge's chambers.

"How do you feel?" Judge Kamata, who was presiding that day, asked me.

"As you see."

"I don't think this experience will be too painful."

"To know whether it is painful or not," I told him, "you must experience it yourself." Too late I realized how impertinent I was, but that really did not matter. Once I was ready for death, the judge was not someone to fear.

"I'm a lawyer, not a man of literature," he said, "so I don't understand this Japanese poem. Now I want to ask a professor of literature to interpret it for me." He handed the poem to me.

"The wide, endless ocean is my theme," I explained. "In the infinite sea, the waves incessantly surge high and disappear. Those huge, billowing breakers hit the big rock and are crushed instantaneously, turning to foam.

"In this metaphor the ocean is history, and the wave is a nation. The waves represent an insane nation that is not able to distinguish between right and wrong. The solid rock is the law of God who created the heavens and the earth and who rules all the universe.

"No matter how powerfully the waves roll in, as soon as they hit the solid rock they are crushed and dissipate into foam. They are made ashamed of themselves before the world and the history of man. The rock is firm and unchanging. The dominion of Jehovah, God, cannot be changed by any power of any nation or race. That is what the poem means."

He listened attentively and was silent for a moment after I finished explaining the meaning of the poem. "You braced yourself for death, didn't you?" he asked.

"I braced myself for death when I gave warning to the Seventy-Fourth Japanese Imperial Diet meeting. I have been dead for six years."

Judge Kamata sighed and ended the interview.

Feeling as refreshed as a clear autumn day, I walked out of his office. I felt like shouting in victory as I lifted my gaze to the high blue sky. My heart sang.

> Hallelujah! The Lord lives.
> He lives with me now. And I love Him only.
> I am a witness of the Lord,
> Hallelujah!

43

THE
REPENTANT
JAILER

When Mrs. Higashi and Kuriyama were transferred to the factory, jailer Jue was placed in charge of the jailers, and new guards were brought in. Their cruelty and hatred darkened their features as they watched me constantly. I was worn out and tired of life. I felt that my only escape was to go to heaven. All day I kept my eyes closed and refused to speak.

"Lord," I prayed, mumbling the words, "I'm so tired. Please call me to heaven. But if nothing else can be done, put an end to my senses so I don't feel anything."

I must admit to feeling very sorry for myself. But as I tried to visualize heaven, joy surged in my heart. I would be among the disciples standing in front of Jesus. How wonderful it would be to see the Lord whom I had been serving in love. Ever since I put my trust in Him to save me, my life and loyalty had been to Him, though I had never seen Him. Now I was approaching the time when I would be able to look up at Him with my own eyes!

The disciples would be there, along with the early church

members and those who had died in the great persecutions in Rome and the rest of the world. We faced hatred and wickedness now, but that gathering would be filled with love, peace, and praise. Such wonderful thoughts made me dread opening my eyes to face the prison's reality.

During this period there was one night that still stands out vividly. Jailer Kane was in charge, and the cell was tense and quiet. Though my eyes were closed, I was sure she was in front of my cell glaring at me.

A world without jailers! That was impossible, except in heaven.

The poetry of Job touched my heart.

As the night wore on, one agonizing minute after another in endless succession, she did not leave my cell. It seemed that she was riveted there. I thought she was giving me a difficult time because I kept my eyes closed.

"Strange," she murmured. At first she spoke so softly that I was not sure I had heard her. Then the word came again clearly. "Strange."

I could not imagine what she was referring to. She went on to the next cell and the next, but soon she was back where she could stare at me.

"It's quite strange," she repeated.

By this time I became aware that there was no anger in her words, though a certain harshness and arrogance crept in. I prayed that God would take me to be with Him that night so I would not have to face the light of morning and the curse it would bring.

When jailer Kane next came on duty, she did not seem as stern as before. Again she stood in front of my cell.

"It's really strange," she said. For the first time I had the impression she was speaking to me. I opened my eyes hesitantly.

"What is strange, Mrs. Kane?" I asked her.

"The faces of people these days. It isn't only in the prisons. It's on the outside, as well. Everybody is nervous and tense and angry. Even the children look wicked. I must confess that the faces of people irritate me. That's why I find this cell so different."

I was surprised and asked her what she meant.

She had difficulty expressing herself. "What shall I say?" she began. "I–I guess it's because I find the faces of those in this cell peaceful."

"Peaceful?" I echoed. *"In here?"*

"That's right. Your face and that of the prisoner in cell three and the one in cell five are all peaceful."

My heart shook off the melancholy that had engulfed it and danced with joy. The ones she mentioned were believers in the Lord Jesus Christ.

She left abruptly, as though she were embarrassed at having made such an observation. I waited impatiently for her to return, and when she did come back I talked with her about it.

"Would you tell me in what way our faces are strange, Mrs. Kane?"

"Well," she began hesitantly, "it almost seems as though you have the faces of angels. And I can't understand it. Nowhere else have I found peaceful faces in this world."

That night a change occurred in our relationship, and I asked if I could talk to her. "You said that our faces look peaceful," I began, "and you said it was strange. Would you like to know why we can look peaceful in such a place as this?"

"Yes," she said, "I want to know about it."

I reminded her of the fact that we were going to be hanged, but even that would not change the peace and serenity in our hearts. We had the joy of Jesus Christ within us.

"Could I be a Christian?" she asked. "I am so sinful."

I had been surprised by her before. Now I was astounded at her confession.

"I think that you are nearly a Christian now," I said to her.

"How can that be?" she asked, "when I am so wicked and sinful?"

"If you were not on the way to becoming a Christian, you probably would not say that you are sinful," I continued.

"Nobody knows she is a sinner unless her sin has been pointed out to her by the Holy Spirit. From now on, just listen to and obey Jesus as you accept Him into your heart."

"How can I do that?" she asked.

"Man can go to God through Jesus Christ. God especially welcomes the sinful, the powerless, the weak, the poor, and the crippled."

She listened to me solemnly. Strengthened, I started speaking of the Bible. As I told her about Zacchaeus and the persecution of Paul and his repentance, she listened earnestly. The night advanced, but that made no difference to either of us.

"Thank you very much, *Sensei* [Teacher]," she said bashfully. Her attitude toward me was completely different from the way it had been. When the time came for her to leave the ward, she came over and told me good-bye. My exhaustion was gone.

From then on I waited anxiously for her to come to work. As long as she was on duty I talked to her.

Before she received Christ as her Savior, her hours of work had dragged by. Now, however, they raced by. She did not eat her lunch but offered it to me, imploring me to take it. I rejoiced at her kindness.

"To tell you the truth," she said one day, "when I was a child I went to Sunday school. Although I did not understand it all, I remember about God and Jesus. But I didn't know how to become a Christian and did not think it was necessary. Now, I am a believer. Even if I would be put into prison like you or hanged for my faith, I would not deny my faith in Him."

The Lord had changed a dreadful jailer, making her my closest protector. She cared and was concerned for me very much, due to her faith. It filled my heart with praise, and the dark prison became bright and happy once more. The Lord lives and works.

44

A DAY
OF REST

A special order was delivered to our cell. Up until that time the prisoners who had been convicted were working at the prison factory, but those who were not yet convicted had nothing whatever to do. All of that was changed by special decree. The unconvicted prisoners were put to work sewing buttons on the military uniforms.

I welcomed the job. My eyes were not good, so I could not do very well at it, but the work made the time pass faster. Until Sunday came. I purposely did not work then.

"Please don't give me a job," I told the Japanese jailer who brought in the materials. "I want to take the day off. I'll work harder on the other days, but on Sunday I would like to rest."

"Who do you think you are?" she demanded. "And where do you think you are?"

"Since I am not convicted yet," I told her calmly, "I am connected with the court. If I am breaking your rules, you are right in informing your superiors. Why don't you report me to them? They will punish me." At first I was deeply frightened, but now I was bold. Although she was very angry, she didn't hit me as I thought she would.

It was only a few moments until the chief jailer was at my cell, furious at my refusal to work on Sunday.

"Your responsibility is to see that I don't escape," I said, confronting her. "I have not yet been convicted. Isn't it your job to inform the officer above you?"

She was so angry that she left quickly. I had talked to her as if I had no fear, but the truth was that I felt sealed off with uneasiness and desperation. Would I be handcuffed again? I could tell by the look on the faces of the jailer and the chief jailer that they were confident I would be tortured. I fully expected it.

"Lord Jesus," I prayed, "save me from the lion."

When I saw their angry faces I could not bear it, so I closed my eyes and began to go over His commandments silently. I was fighting for my life over the commandments of the Law.

I would have to obey the first commandment and the fourth, as I loved and trusted God. If one commandment was broken, all were broken.

I refused my meals that day, and all night I prayed, waiting for His will and judgment. Once the matter was resolved, I would listen to and obey His commandments at all cost. It was the will of my love for God, but my weakness was not changed. Fear and apprehension afflicted me.

"O Father in heaven, I am afraid. Please hide me beneath Your wings."

At dawn I went to sleep and dreamed of Sumo wrestlers in a big playground waiting in line to begin wrestling. Their huge bellies were like mountains. The wrestlers seemed to be waiting for me. I appeared with two-edged swords and, one after another, suddenly I ran to them and quickly pierced their enormous bellies. They all fell and didn't get up again. Singing "Allelupah," I woke up. My faith was steadfast on the foundation of

God's love. It was as if I were on my way to raid the enemy headquarters. I got up and worshiped the Lord.

"Number 57, come out!" the chief woman jailer shouted. Leaving my cell, I saw the apprehensive faces of my fellow prisoners.

The chief jailer was confident and triumphant, taking me to the office of the commandant. The wide room was luxurious and impressive. When we entered, everyone in the room wore uniforms that blazed with stripes and gold buttons. I was so preoccupied with the luxury of the office that I forgot to greet the commandant. But since I was a prisoner, I don't suppose my greeting would have counted for very much anyway.

I was neither fearful nor apprehensive. In fact, I was so calm and at peace that I was surprised at myself.

"I understand that you are well educated and have a good measure of common sense," he said, "but you still rebel by ignoring the rules. Tell me, is that true?"

"Do you know that I am here without a crime?" I asked him.

"That has nothing to do with the matter. You must have committed some crime or you wouldn't be in prison. And once you are here, there are rules that you have to obey."

"Because of my faith I have been humiliated," I told him. "Keeping my faith is most important to me in spite of the fact that it brings tribulation. That is the reason I am here."

He was as angry at me as the chief jailer had ever been. "In this time of emergency you are stubborn. The entire nation is trying to win this holy war. How long are you going to be afflicted with your madness and insist upon your mistaken concepts?"

"Commandant," I said quietly, "have I neglected the rules of the prison? Have I broken them purposely? I should not be a prisoner, but as a prisoner I have obeyed the rules faithfully. But I cannot disobey my faith, and I will not, no matter how much you insist on it."

Then he stood quickly and slammed his fist against his

desk. "As the faithful servant of the great imperial Japanese emperor and the commandant of the Pyongyang prison, I order you to serve the nation by doing your work every day."

Usually I tried to control myself. This time I was as furious as he was. I rushed to his side and hit the desk with my small fist as hard as he had done.

"As a servant of God who created the heavens and the earth and overrules the whole world, I cannot obey rules that ignore the rules of God." My soprano voice was strained, my fists were hot like Hades, and my throat burned. He seemed stunned and astonished by the sudden anger that swept over me. Dropping his voice, he asked me to sit down.

I did so, whispering in my heart, *You fat Sumo wrestler. You are dead by the two-edged sword.*

I was not prepared for what he had to say. "The God you believe in saved you today."

The room was silent. Watching the tense tableau, the section chief and the department head seemed to be robbed of the ability to move. They stared at me, their pale faces darkening. Vexed by my outburst and the commandant's reaction, the chief woman jailer was trembling. Only I was calm.

"I am already dead," I told them. "The fact that I am alive now depends on the love of Christ. I will soon be executed."

He groaned and turned to the chief jailer. "Don't pick on this young lady too much," he said. "Every instruction will be issued by the court. Do you understand?"

"Yes, commandant, sir."

I could not help being sorry for her. I got to my feet and left the office. No one spoke. The chief jailer walked behind me, her anger smoldering.

From the square courtyard I looked up at the sky.

"The Lord lives!" I said aloud. Then, although everyone was watching, I knelt on the ground and worshiped God. In my heart a beautiful orchestra was praising God, and as we walked briskly to the prison a few moments later I had an impulse to sing my favorite hymns.

At the chief jailer's office, she exploded belligerently. "That commandant was crazy! He was completely provoked by a young woman!"

I was sorry for her. Those who did not know God could be expected to make the wrong interpretation.

After the confrontation with the commandant, I did not work on Sundays but spent my time with the Lord. If we did not rest, how miserable we would be, with no difference between ourselves and the beasts. Because of His fatherly love, God consecrated the Sabbath day to make us rest. I was grateful for it.

45

THE WORLD
TURNED OVER

It was August 15, 1945, when jailer Jue came on duty with some startling news.

"Japan has signed an unconditional surrender!"

Word raced through the ward. It was all but impossible to believe.

"Japan is defeated!" she repeated. "She has surrendered unconditionally, and Korea is free!"

"Who is saying all this?" I demanded.

"The jailers are all talking about it, and there are no officers around anywhere." Excitement gripped her. "The Japanese staff is gone! Not one is on duty this morning!"

I was as shocked as the others. At first I felt as though I were dreaming. Then, I, too, was swept up in the excitement of the moment. The world had suddenly turned upside down. Controlling my emotion, I praised, thanked, and worshiped the Lord. Then I called out to Mrs. Jue to open the cells.

"I will unlock cells one, three, and five," she said. Those of us in those cells were imprisoned for our faith. We were not criminals.

We were so excited that we grasped each others' hands and tried to dance. I'm sure it would have been amusing for anyone who had seen us. We didn't know how to dance, and we already were so tired that we tottered feebly. Still we jumped around as well as we could.

I was probably more bewildered than anyone else. I had been considering myself dead for so long. And especially the last few weeks. Now I was free!

Pandemonium had taken over the women's ward. There was no iron fist to keep the prisoners quiet. Those who were still in their cells were shouting for freedom and banging at their doors, trying to get out.

Soon the noon meal arrived. Never, in all the years I had been imprisoned, had I seen such a meal. The rice looked as though it had come from some luxurious cafe, and there was a tantalizing side dish. But, hungry as we were, no one even tried to eat it at first. When we did sit down to eat, it was as tasteless to us as so much sand. The excitement robbed it of its flavor.

Our very beings were filled with an indescribable joy. It was particularly surprising to us because we had been kept completely ignorant of the war's progress. Now we were about to be loosed from the chains of the Japanese, our cruel persecutors for thirty-seven years, and to be freed from prison as well.

"No more shrine worship!" the prisoners were shouting.

"No more draft."

"No more Japanese names."

"No more speaking in Japanese to get rations."

"We can praise the American planes as we wish and nobody will arrest us."

"We'll get our land back and everything!"

Again at suppertime another huge meal was brought to us, but nobody wanted to eat. And at night no one wanted to go to sleep. In fact, sleep was impossible. Everyone was shouting and talking until dawn.

The next morning jailer Kuriyama came to tell me more. The Japanese emperor had gone on the radio to announce that Japan had surrendered unconditionally to America and her allies. The Japanese had even burned their shrines with kerosene. "So, Miss Ahn, you won't see shrines anywhere when you get out. They used to consider their shrines as sacred. Now they are ashamed of them as if they are something dirty. You won't see any Japanese on the street. They are all in their homes, afraid to come out." She smiled at the thought. "They were so proud, but now they look and act like slaves. They are begging for forgiveness."

Although the cells in which we three believers were held had been opened for a time, we had been returned to them. We were anxious to be released, but it was almost two days before we were. Around 11 P.M. on August 17, 1945, our cells were opened. We Christians were the first to be set free. Jailer Kuriyama and Jue walked on either side of me, supporting me as we walked down a long hall. Passing the women's prison and approaching the main gate, I saw the surviving male Christian prisoners also leaving the prison.

When we were all together just inside the gate, the jailer in charge shouted for attention. "Ladies and gentlemen! These are the ones who for six long years refused to worship Japanese gods. They fought against severe torture, hunger, and cold, and have won out without bowing their heads to the idol worship of Japan. Today they are the champions of faith!"

Suddenly the throng of people outside the gate shouted as one. "Praise the name of Jesus!"

A hymn was sung:

> All hail the power of Jesus' name!
> Let angels prostrate fall.
> Bring forth the royal diadem
> And crown Him Lord of all.
>
> JAMES ELLOR

Then the gate was opened, and the crowd outside saluted us as we started moving out. Each family had prepared a rickshaw for us, and we all were able to ride in a long, triumphant procession.

My sister didn't wait but ran to me, and I soon found my mother. Our hearts were crying with joy and thanksgiving as we sang our praises to our God.

The great city of Pyongyang rang with the hymns of praise and joy that night as thousands joined their voices and marched through the city.

Our praise to the Lord awakened those who were still in their homes.

When we reached our house, everyone stopped. Although the building was large, it could not accommodate all the people, so they surrounded it. The tables almost collapsed under the weight of the food that had been prepared, but no one attempted to eat. The released Christians looked at each other and offered thanks to God for everything that had happened. We freed believers were heroes. We were regarded as great men and women of history because of the way we had stood up to the Japanese, but we were all humble, staying in the shadow of Jesus. Thirty-four Christians had entered Pyongyang prison. Only fourteen survived.

Dawn came, but still the people did not go home. At noon, one young woman came running to me.

"Miss Ahn!" she called out. "I'm Sun Wha!"

My eyes were not good enough to allow me to see who she was, but I recognized her voice. With great joy I grabbed her hands. They were callused and rough.

"I went to a deep mountain valley and became an evangelist there," she told me in response to my question about her hands. "It's just a poor mountainous village with very poor peasants." She had taught the children to read and sing and told them about Jesus Christ.

I was so moved I could find no words to tell her of my happiness. She went on to tell me that she had made me some candies.

"I remembered that you wanted candies so much when you were in prison," she explained.

It was difficult for me to believe that, just as she had promised me in prison, she had become a woman evangelist. We praised the Lord together.

People were constantly visiting me. We sang hymns together and worshiped the Lord all the time.

"They that trust in Jehovah are as mount Zion, which cannot be moved, but abideth for ever" (Psalm 125:1).

"When Jehovah brought back those that returned to Zion, we were like unto them that dream. Then was our mouth filled with laughter, and our tongue with singing. . . . Jehovah hath done great things for us, whereof we are glad" (Psalm 126:1–3).

46

MILLIONAIRE STREET SWEEPERS

I went to the court accompanied by several young men to see Judge Kamata. He welcomed me politely and asked me to sit down. Although he had sentenced me to death for breaking the Japanese law, he had shown sympathy toward me. Unofficially he had been very human and friendly. I didn't know why.

I was the first to speak, asking him what he was going to do now that the war was over.

"I don't know," he answered. "I just don't know."

"I came to thank you for helping me when I was in trouble," I said. "I have never been able to be of much help to you, but I would like to help you in an eternal way."

I thought he seemed interested. "What do you mean?"

"As you know, I am a Christian," I began. "I would like you to become a believer in Jesus Christ. I would like you to have an encounter with God."

"I understand what you're saying," he told me. "In order to investigate Christians I had to read the Bible. I am beginning to understand it in another sense." He spoke nervously and I sensed a strong feeling that the conversation should continue no further.

Leaving his chambers, I recalled the days when the chief jailer ordered my hands cuffed behind me and pulled down by a heavy iron ball at the end of a chain. There had been no relief from the agony either day or night. I was forced to endure the pain which pierced my chest and body. At the memory, I broke out in a cold sweat.

It was then that Judge Kamata visited me. I could still feel him standing in front of my cell, watching me. The very next morning my chains were removed. There was no angel in hell, but I was in hell and he played the angel. My present visit with him gave me the feeling that I had finished my unfinished task. Judge Kamata was killed by a bomb during the Korean War after being imprisoned for five years by Communists (1945–50) prior to the outbreak of hostilities.

The next day in downtown Pyongyang I was startled to see Japanese sweeping the city. They were wearing headbands and were in their traditional *yukata* (summer clothes). *The strong become weak,* I thought, *and the servants become strong.* Our former masters were sweeping the city. The city commissioner was one of those with a broom. Another was a well-known millionaire store owner, while still another was the principal of the largest high school in the city.

Many Koreans were sympathetic and kindly, but many others were bitter and belligerent. "Look at them!" they snarled, shaking their fists. "For forty years they squeezed our blood and made themselves fat. Now look where they are!"

"They killed my parents with severe torture," an unforgiving young man said. "How God has punished them."

The educated seemed to understand and sympathize with the Japanese, but the poor believed that all their poverty and troubles were caused by the Japanese. They considered our former rulers as their enemies.

The Japanese were forced to turn over all their property to the Koreans. Their fortunes, their land, everything had to be turned over to our people. Though they once had been wealthy, they were now beggars.

In extreme apprehension, the Japanese seemed to be waiting for instructions from their homeland. Rumor had it that some Japanese who had mastered our language well disguised themselves as Koreans. The most unfortunate were the married couples who had to be separated because one or the other was Japanese. I could not help crying for them.

I had thought the Japanese would be wise enough to come to their senses once they saw that their gods did not have the power to save them. When the emperor himself announced to the world that he was only a man and not a god, I was sure we would see Japan turn to the true God, the Creator and Ruler of the heavens and the earth.

Surely they would welcome Jesus Christ, the Son of God, and become examples for all of Asia. Then tomorrow would be a splendid day in the history of mankind. Only the Gospel of Jesus could turn man's hatred into love, his enemies into brothers. By sharing the Gospel and being under the love of Jesus, it would be possible to establish peace.

Every day when I was downtown I would see a throng of Japanese marching in lines as they were returning to Japan. None had any luggage. They only possessed the clothes they were wearing. Each person was holding one small, empty can. They were all apprehensive and looked as though they were on the verge of collapsing from exhaustion and hunger.

"Where do these people come from?" one Korean asked me. "How can Japan accommodate so many people?"

I wanted to give them food, but I could not. There were too many of them.

The Japanese we were seeing were not just those who had been in Korea before the war's end. Others from Manchuria and continental China were passing through our nation on their way home. High officials, such as Judge Kamata and the gestapo police, were captured by the Communist party members. They were being tortured and sentenced just as they had done to the Christians.

"Fret not thyself because of evil-doers, neither be thou envious against them that work unrighteousness. For they shall soon be cut down like the grass, and wither as the green herb" (Psalm 37:1–2).

Brimstone fire had finally fallen on Japan. It was delivered by American B-29s raining incendiary bombs on Tokyo, Yokohama, Osaka, Nagoya, and all the other major cities. It had come, too, in the horror of the atomic bombs dropped on Hiroshima and Nagasaki.

Fires were everywhere. Entire cities were in flames.

"I was in Tokyo during the bombing," a young man from that city told me. "I've never seen such a living hell. Nobody was crying out from pain or sorrow. People ran around senselessly even when they saw the shelters. Human bodies were charred and blackened like coal. Without God, human beings are like dead flies without feelings or sympathy or love."

I thought back to the time when God had called me to go to Japan to warn the nation. At that time the Japanese were strong and confident. When I had looked down from the seventh floor of the Tokyo hotel I could never have imagined that the nation would ever fall or that the confidence of the Japanese would be shaken. I was like a solitary sea gull trying to calm the angry waves.

After my friend told me about the bombings, I felt ashamed of myself for having doubted that God would accomplish His word. I thought of those who had made fun of me. What were they doing now? Did they remember God's warning? And the proud and boastful leaders—the commander, the torturers, the politicians—what were they thinking now?

I had learned the lesson that God does what He says He will do. My heart ached for the many Japanese who had died without hearing the Gospel. Many opportunities had been lost to tell them of Christ, opportunities that could never be retrieved. I felt deep regret.

KIDNAPPED
BY THE
COMMUNISTS

Every day Russian trucks filled with soldiers arrived in the city of Pyongyang. The short-necked Russian soldiers with their husky bodies and their faces scarred and reddened with pimples were an ignorant lot. Their lack of education was stamped on their coarse features.

They had only one thing on their minds when their convoys stopped in the center of the city: women. Burning with lust, they fanned out through the streets, seeking any female within reach. It mattered not to them whether their victims were grandmothers or flat-chested grade school girls. Even the fact that it was daylight did not stop them. They seized their victims and committed their atrocities right in the streets, like so many ravishing dogs.

The relief from Japan's oppression had given way to the terror of the bestial behavior of the Russian soldiers. In their mad search for women to rape, they looted every home they came to. One Russian soldier stole a watch for the pleasure of hearing it tick. He could not tell time, nor did he know how to wind it, so when it stopped he threw it away and stole another.

I wondered if they had any moral code or if they had ever received any military training. They were all armed and quick to kill anyone who did not communicate well or was not quick enough in replying to suit them.

The stories we heard were horrible. When a large group of soldiers caught a lone woman, they formed a line to rape her. She died under their inhuman abuse.

Early in the morning the sound of gunshots could be heard all over the city. The houses had to be locked and the women hid in shelters, not daring to go out at all. The men did the chores. Every time a gun sounded, it meant somebody was being killed. There was no moment of relief. Everyone had to wander around in the darkness.

After two months the news spread that the soldiers who had wrought such havoc in Pyongyang were not regular soldiers but prisoners who had volunteered to fight. Soon they were returned home, and the regular Russian soldiers arrived.

We were relieved and thought that peace and order were about to be restored. Young men of the Red Party were distributing Russian flags and ordering us out to welcome the Russian soldiers. Curious about them, I went downtown with a flag in hand and awaited their arrival. Soon I heard the voices of robust men singing, and truckloads of soldiers appeared. The citizens waved the flags and were impressed with the singing.

I watched the long parade.

We had been assured that the regular army would be under better control, but there was little difference. They picked up where the prison rabble left off, raping women and looting homes and shops. The Korean Communist Party members rode in their jeeps with them, proud to be a part of the Communist regime.

It wasn't long until the 38th parallel was established as the northern limit of American influence. North of that line the Russians were to be in control. Most of the people were apprehensive and afraid, and a growing exodus began as people started south to escape to the part of the country that was governed by the Americans. It mattered to few Koreans that they had to give up property, homes, and even their villages. Entire families fled, carrying whatever they could. Soon the Russians established a heavy guard along the 38th parallel and began to shoot down refugees who attempted to cross over.

"How many more times will we be cursed?" we wondered. Darkness and agony persisted. Mother and I were both exhausted.

The day came when we were visited by the Communists. Mr. Ju, the youthful Communist member who had been in prison at the same time as I was, was one of them. One of the women accompanying him was a Russian officer. The other was a Miss Park who had been in prison with me. At the time she was in my cell she looked like an ignorant merchant woman, but now she was haughty and arrogant.

"It's so nice to see you, Miss Ahn," Miss Park said. "You were so bold in fighting against the Japanese. Your spirit of patriotism is truly reverent and beautiful."

She grasped my hand so firmly I could not free myself of her grip.

I was ready to break out in anger, but I managed to control myself.

"Let's stand up," Park said, ignoring my feelings. "The time has come. The Japanese who were poisonous snakes, have gone. It's time for us to be strict with the people."

"Miss Ahn," Ju said, recalling our conversations during the period when we were jailed, "you wanted to go to heaven when you die. We are going to show you heaven while you are alive. Since Moscow is living heaven, we are going to take you there by special plane."

He explained at length that Moscow was, indeed, heaven on earth. Sensing that I was burning with indignation, they continued to speak Russian. I didn't understand them at all and didn't wish to know what they were saying.

They left after a time, but in three days Park and the Russian woman officer were back.

"We are having a special party tonight, Miss Ahn," she said. "We must ask that you be there. We have come to pick you up. This was supposed to have been Mr. Ju's task, but he couldn't make it, so he sent me. There will be a dinner tonight, so please bring your mother."

At first she was kind about our refusal, but then she was persistent and, in the end, threatening. Since I had no valid excuse, I was forced to get into the jeep. Thinking that I was being kidnapped, I was terribly frightened.

"O Lord," I prayed in silence, "help me. Rescue me."

I could not pray more. She talked to me constantly.

The jeep climbed up Nam San Hill where Russian soldiers were very much in evidence. As we passed by, the guards saluted us.

At the house where we stopped, there were more guards than usual. We went into a large living room with a long sofa along one side and a round table in the center. The female officer soon left us, and Park asked me to sit down amid the luxury.

"You're the first to come," she commented. "Soon everybody else will show up." She didn't tell me what she meant by everybody. She seemed preoccupied and said she had to make a phone call.

As soon as she was gone, I decided to leave in my bare feet by way of the backyard. Reciting the Scripture, "Be strong and very courageous" (Joshua 1:7 NASB), I left the room and went into the rest room. From there I went into the garden and walked along the back garden of the house next door. I soon came to an alley where a few people were walking about. I ran, but as soon as I saw someone I walked, being careful to cover my bare feet with my long skirt.

When I reached the main street, I saw that a Russian soldier was standing in front of each house. Controlling my nervous heart and pretending there was nothing wrong, I passed a Russian soldier. He looked at me suspiciously.

Once I was some distance away from the house, I didn't care for anything anymore. I just kept running.

It was too far to go to my own home so I headed for Elder Yun's house. I was gasping for air and my heart was beating furiously.

Somebody was running with me. I didn't know who it was, but suddenly I realized that it was Jesus Himself. My heart sang and my spirit was lifted up. I ran with joy.

When I arrived at Elder Yun's, the gate was securely locked. I called out loudly to him and banged at the gate with both hands. When it opened, I pushed a servant aside and rushed into the house.

When I had calmed down somewhat, I told Mr. and Mrs. Yun everything. They were amazed. "One cannot escape from the Communist party members. Surely God granted you wisdom," they said.

I asked Elder Yun to get my mother to his house as quickly as possible. He sent several husky young men for her. She came with a large Bible and several changes of clothes. Realizing that it was very dangerous now for us to remain in Pyongyang, we all knelt down before the Lord, asking for His guidance.

FREEDOM
AT LAST!

That night Elder Yun called together a group of Christian young men and told them how I had been kidnapped by the Communists. Everybody was shocked. It was obvious that my situation was increasingly dangerous and that the only course open for me was to cross the 38th parallel and head for Seoul.

"Can someone help Miss Ahn?" he asked.

Immediately ten young men volunteered to lead me on the perilous trip.

My sister's son-in-law was visiting us from the south, but, because of the 38th parallel decision, it had been impossible for him to return home. So he was happy to join us. The total number of the party was fourteen. Instilled with the sense of a mission, these men were ready to help me.

"We don't mind being killed getting you across the parallel," the men said.

Mother and I could not help but cry. The ten men carried the packages which my sister brought. Among the men was one who was called "Brave Bull." He became the leader of the group. His older brother was not as strong, but, because of his faith, he was going anyway. To me, every young man looked strong and sturdy. They were all excited at the prospect of going on this adventure. Somehow I felt that all fourteen of us became as one. We gathered in a large room and ate a sumptuous dinner. Praising God and singing hymns to Him, we waited until one o'clock in the morning. Then we all stood up and, in ones and twos, left the house for the train station. Once on the train, we sat where we could see each other. The train was crowded with people fleeing to the south.

The next morning we had to eat breakfast, but there was no such thing as a restaurant nearby, so we went to a house on the edge of the road and paid the owners for preparing a meal for us. After resting for a time, we formed a single file and headed for the south.

Many children and women were walking slowly and separately, so that if Russian soldiers or Communist party members came by, an entire family would not be captured and sent back. Brave Bull questioned a merchant, who had crossed the border and returned many times on business, in order to find out the easiest place to cross as well as the most successful way to do it.

I prayed relentlessly, recalling the troubled days when I was in prison and had no freedom. The brotherly love among these men was certainly a great manifestation of God's mercy. As night came, Brave Bull hired a wagon that was pulled by a cow. The men walked and we three women rode.

A quarter moon was in the sky, and dark clouds hovered around it, symbolizing the danger of our trip. I gathered all my strength and recited chapter 14 of the Gospel of John. Keeping rhythm with the wheels of the wagon, I sang a hymn. The others all kept praying.

Suddenly the man who drove the wagon stopped and refused to go on. We were close to the 38th parallel and going farther would be very dangerous.

"As soon as the Russians hear the wheels of the wagon, they will shoot us," he said.

We three women got off and walked in silence, one step after another. By this time it was raining heavily. Thunder roared and lightning flashed across the sky. We had worn dark clothing in order to help us escape being detected, and lightning lit up the area. Our vision was hampered as we proceeded on our way without knowing where we were. There was no road. Sometimes we stumbled, but we kept going, leaning on the hand of the Lord.

We listened to the sounds of rain in the dark night, and our clothing became soaked. A cock crowed somewhere, and that seemed to be an indication of hope for us, but we could not be slack. The only way we could go was forward. Eventually the rain stopped, and at the same time we could see the eastern sky. Through a break in the clouds, we saw beautiful rays of light.

"Hallelujah! Hallelujah!" we shouted for joy as we thanked God. Then we realized, gratefully, that we had already crossed the 38th parallel. While we were crossing the 38th parallel, heavy rain had been falling. Because of the rain, the Russian soldiers were unable to see us. They could not even have known where they were supposed to be themselves. We went wild in jubilation.

I sang "Hallelujah" from Handel's *Messiah*. Musician Cho, my sister's son-in-law, joined in, his rich tenor filling the early morning air. Then all the others sang too. The singing of that choir sounded over the mountains, meadows, and streams. I recalled what the Bible said about the parting of the Red Sea.

We were not alone in crossing the 38th parallel and moving south. Some were happy because of their new freedom. Others were sad to have left their native villages and homes. Others were furious at the Russians and the Communists. There were those who had lost their families and were weeping.

One family had undergone a particularly tense situation. The mother was carrying her baby. When the rain began to fall, the baby cried and the frightened mother held her so tightly that she almost suffocated.

Some thought they had crossed the 38th parallel, but in the morning they found that they merely had been walking in circles.

Brave Bull negotiated for a truck, and we all got on it to ride south. As soon as we got on, we started singing again, thanking the living God.

It wasn't long until we saw our first American soldiers. They were stopping all vehicles on the road in a thorough inspection for weapons and troublemakers. We didn't quit singing when they stopped us. A soldier with a rifle in his hand smiled and waved us on. Our singing became more and more cheerful. We had crossed the Red Sea and finally reached the land of Canaan.

AMERICA

There was a great number of refugees from the north when we arrived in Seoul. Long lines of men, women, and children, with the few clothes and personal possessions they could carry, were streaming into the city. Confusion reigned.

The young men who went south with us took us to the home of Elder Yun's daughter. As soon as they learned that there were two empty rooms in the big house which we could rent, they said good-bye and left to return home.

Our friend's daughter was a devout believer, which made it very nice for us. And the house was so large that we could have complete privacy whenever we wanted it.

It was then that I set to work, writing in my diary. For six years I had not been able to do so. Now I recalled everything that had happened to me from the day I quit teaching school until the day I was freed from the Japanese. I seemed compelled by some force outside myself to write down everything, including my innermost thoughts and desires. From early morning until late at night I kept writing.

During this period an acquaintance asked if I would be interested in teaching home economics at Sook Myring Women's University. My major had been home economics, but I had never taught the subject. My real interest was in music and literature, so for that reason I turned down the offer.

It wasn't long until my friend was back again, asking me to teach music at a girls' school. However, I had not practiced the piano for over seven years and my voice was much lower than it had been before my imprisonment. In addition, my confidence and physical condition were not good. I would not be able to do an acceptable job of teaching the subject.

About that same time a beautiful American woman accompanied by an interpreter visited me. She introduced herself as Phyllis Coe. She told me that I was very famous in the United States and she wanted to meet me. I thought she had come to visit me by mistake.

"You're Miss Ahn, aren't you?" she asked.

After we talked for a few minutes, she explained the purpose of her visit. She asked me if I would like to go to America.

I had always wanted to go to America. For a long while I thought I should have gone there instead of going to Japan. Now my health was not good, and I did not want to leave my mother.

"You don't have to stay very long," she said. "We would like to have you travel around America giving your testimony for a period of three months."

My mother encouraged me, and my new American friend gave me a check for a thousand dollars. My mind was made up.

During my years in prison, the Japanese government had driven all the American missionaries from Korea. Among them was a medical doctor who with his wife had previously served in Manchuria. They refused to leave Korea and were put in prison and tortured along with the other Christians. At the peak of the shrine worship, they had visited Pyongyang. They arrived about the same time I returned after warning the Tokyo government. They heard my testimony when a group of the remaining missionaries met secretly. Both the doctor and his wife were impressed by it. They also learned that I was imprisoned later.

The devout couple were on the last exchange ship to America after having been imprisoned for a year. As soon as they arrived home, they wrote a pamphlet entitled "If I perish, I perish." It told how I was called by God to go to Japan and give a message of warning at the Seventy-fourth Diet meeting, and how I was arrested and imprisoned for it. This pamphlet was distributed widely among believers in America. A wealthy Southerner was so impressed by it that he had it reprinted for distribution across the United States, Canada, England, Australia, and South America.

Phyllis was one of those who read the pamphlet. After much prayer she came to Korea and, with a thousand dollars in her hand, asked me to come to America to give my testimony.

About that time a young man by the name of Kim Dong Myung visited me. He had graduated from an engineering college in Kobe and worked in Tokyo, designing tunnels and bridges. Afterward he returned to Korea and studied civil engineering at the University of Seoul. He had been given a scholarship from the United States and had already finished preparations for a doctor's degree at MIT. More important, he was burning with God's love.

Years before, my mother had encouraged me to be a pastor's wife. I had insisted I would not marry a pastor. My husband, I said, would have to be an engineer. Mother and I had competed against each other in our prayers. We both laughed at our predicament.

I had my way by marrying an engineer, but God did not allow the matter to rest there. My husband decided to abandon his chosen profession and become a pastor. With God's help, Mother won out, but by this time I was as eager as he that he serve the Lord full time.

When I went to the American embassy to apply for my visa, I was asked if I understood and spoke English well.

"I don't speak it at all," I confessed.

"What would you do if you went to the English-speaking world and couldn't speak the language?" the ambassador asked me.

I didn't like the tenor of his questioning. I was not surprised but was deeply disappointed when he told me that since I did not speak English, it would be better for me not to go.

I thanked him and left his office. Just outside the door I met an old friend, an American missionary I had not seen for years. I told Reverend Edward Adams that I was sad when I heard that he had been expelled from Korea.

"As soon as I heard the war was over," he said, "I came back." Then he said that he had heard I survived my own imprisonment and that he had wanted to see me but had not known where to locate me. I told him about the diary I was writing and the decision to go to America.

"But I was refused a visa," I said.

"Would you like to see the ambassador again?" he asked. "I'll go with you and explain how things are."

The ambassador seemed to know the missionary very well. They talked for a time, and I was sure that I was the subject of their conversation. The ambassador's expression changed. When the conversation stopped, he bowed to me in the Oriental manner, his eyes clouded with tears.

"Since the ambassador didn't know about you," Reverend Adams said, "he did not treat you with the respect you deserve. He apologizes for it and he says that you can go to America and give your testimony."

With the treasured visa in my hand, we went to the reservations office of an airline. One plane was leaving for America each month, and the next would leave the following day. He checked the passenger list. Yes, there was a seat available.

Once my mind was made up, everything went easily. All the Christians gathered that night in a farewell party for me. I told Mother that I would be away for three months and that I did not want her going to heaven while I was gone.

"Now that you have a chance to go to America," she told me, "make the most of the opportunity. Maybe it will be God's will that we see each other again at the gate of heaven."

That was the last time I ever saw her.

My plane stopped briefly at Tokyo and I saw that the once-great city had been hammered flat, just as God had told me it would be. Suddenly I felt the fear of Almighty God who had brought judgment upon a nation which was warned, yet did not repent. I also feared the judgment that would come upon every people and nation that continued to rebel against Almighty God.

Japan had suffered greatly in showers of brimstone fire. I wondered how they felt about the pride of idol worship while they had been burning in the fire. The reality was frightening. I prayed to God for the beaten and miserable people of Japan. I prayed that they would open their hearts to the Gospel, listen to the message of salvation, and accept the Lord and be saved. They would no longer covet wealth and power, and they would be free of greed, thinking of the poor as their brothers. My plane flew high over the ocean toward a new world—America. My singing praises continued in the sky.

"O God, Thou art living! I love Thee more than ever before!"